Critters

of Iowa

Pocket Guide to Animals in Your State

ALEX
TROUTMAN

produced in cooperation with
Wildlife Forever

About Wildlife Forever

Wildlife Forever works to conserve America's outdoor heritage through conservation education, preservation of habitat, and scientific management of fish and wildlife. Wildlife Forever is a 501c3 nonprofit organization dedicated to restoring habitat and teaching the next generation about conservation. Become a member and learn more about innovative programs like the Art of Conservation®, The Fish and Songbird Art Contests®, Clean Drain Dry Initiative™, and Prairie City USA®. For more information, visit wildlifeforever.org.

Thank you to Ann McCarthy, the original creator of the Critters series, for her dedication to wildlife conservation and to environmental education. Ann dedicates her work to her daughters, Megan and Katharine Anderson.

Front cover photos by **Steve Byland/shutterstock.com:** spring peeper, **Ayman Haykal/shutterstock.com:** eastern fox squirrel, **Kevin Manns/shutterstock.com:** yellow-billed cuckoo; Back cover photo by **Jim Cumming/Shutterstock.com:** red fox

Edited by Brett Ortler and Jenna Barron
Cover and book design by Jonathan Norberg
Proofreader: Emily Beaumont

10 9 8 7 6 5 4 3 2 1

Critters of Iowa
First Edition 2003, Second Edition 2024

Published by Adventure Publications
An imprint of AdventureKEEN
310 Garfield Street South, Cambridge, Minnesota 55008
(800) 678-7006
www.adventurepublications.net
Printed in China
Cataloging-in-Publication data is available from the Library of Congress
ISBN 978-1-64755-353-1 (pbk.); 978-1-64755-354-8 (ebook)

Acknowledgments

I want to thank everyone who believed in and supported me over the years—a host of friends, family, and teachers. I want to especially thank my mom and my siblings Van, Bre, and TJ.

Dedication

I dedicate this book to my brother Van:
May you continue to enjoy the birds and wildlife in heaven.

This book is for all the kids who have a passion for nature and the outdoors, especially ones who identify as Black, Brown, Indigenous, and People of Color. May this be an encouragement to never give up. And if you have a dream and passion for something, pursue it relentlessly. I also hope to set an example that you can be your full, authentic self!

Lastly, I dedicate this book to all those with ADHD, dyslexia, and all other members of the neurodivergent community. While our quirks make things more challenging, our goals are not impossible to reach; sometimes it takes a little more time and help, but we, too, can succeed!

Contents

Reptiles and Amphibians

Introduction

My passion for nature started when I was young. I was always amazed by the sunlit fiery glow of the red-tailed hawks as they soared overhead when I went fishing with my family. The red-tailed hawk was my spark bird—the bird that captures your attention and gets you into birding. Through my many encounters with red-tailed hawks, and other species like garter snakes and coyotes, I found a passion for nature and the environment. Stumbling across conservationists like Steve Irwin, Jeff Corwin, and Jack Hanna introduced me to the field of Wildlife Biology as a career and gave birth to a dream that I was able to accomplish and live out: serving as a Fish and Wildlife Biologist for governmental agencies, as well as in the private sector.

My childhood dream was driven by a desire to learn more about the different types of ecosystems and the animals that call our wild places home. Books and field guides like this one whet my thirst for knowledge. Even before I could fully understand the words on the pages, I was drawn to books and flashcards that had animals on them. I could identify every animal I was shown and tell a fact about it. I hope that this edition of *Critters of Iowa* can be the fuel that sustains your passion for not only learning about wildlife, but also for caring for the environment and making sure that all are welcome in the outdoors. For others, may this book be the spark that ignites a flame for wildlife preservation and environmental stewardship. I hope that this book inspires children from lower socioeconomic and minority backgrounds to pursue their dreams to the fullest and be unapologetically themselves.

By profession, I'm a Fish and Wildlife Biologist, and I'm a nature enthusiast through and through. My love for nature includes making sure that everyone has an equal opportunity to enjoy the outdoors in their own way. So, as you use this book, I encourage you to be intentional in inviting others to enjoy nature with you. Enjoy your discoveries and stay curious!

–Alex Troutman

Iowa: The Hawkeye State

Iowa is known for its farmlands, producing more corn than any other state. Iowa was first home to several Indigenous tribes including the Dakota, Otoe, Ioway, and others. Europeans came to the area in the 1600s; the land was fought over by the Spanish and French for the next century. Iowa became part of the United States through the Louisiana Purchase in 1803 and became the 29th state in the year 1846.

Iowa is in the midwestern United States and has three geological areas. In the north and central part of the state, the Young Drift Plains are the flat area that is known for its agriculture as well as lakes and swamps. "Drift" is the soil that is made up of clay, sand, rocks, and gravel, likely coming from the glaciers of the Ice Age more than 12,000 years ago. In northeastern Iowa, the Driftless Area has pine forests, hills, and cliffs. Finally, in southern Iowa, the Dissected Till Plains stretch all the way to the northwestern part of the state. It is called "dissected" because rivers have cut into the land, creating the hilly landscape of ridges and bluffs.

These environments are home to many animals, including 72 species of mammals, more than 400 species of birds, and around 70 species of reptiles and amphibians, not to mention fish, countless insects and spiders, mushrooms, plants, and more. This is your guide to the animals, birds, reptiles, and amphibians that call Iowa home.

Some of Iowa's most iconic plants, animals, and other natural resources are now officially recognized as state symbols. Get to know them below and see if you can spot them all! You'll probably encounter the state nickname—the Hawkeye state—and motto, which is listed below.

State Bird:
American goldfinch

State Rock:
geode

State Tree:
bur oak

State Flower:
wild rose

State Motto:
"Our liberties we prize and our rights we will maintain."

How to Use This Guide

This book is your introduction to some of the wonderful critters found in Iowa; it includes 22 mammals, 25 birds, and 17 reptiles and amphibians. It includes some animals you probably already know, such as deer and bald eagles, but others you may not know about, such as plains spadefoot toads or yellow-billed cuckoos. I've selected the species in this book because they are widespread (American badger, page 12), abundant (blue jay, page 68), or well-known but best observed from a safe distance (timber rattlesnake, page 134).

The book is organized by type of animals: mammals, birds, and reptiles and amphibians. Within each section, the animals are in alphabetical order. If you'd like to look for a critter quickly, turn to the checklist (page 140), which you can also use to keep track of how many animals you've seen! For each species, you'll see a photo of the animal, along with neat facts and information on the animal's habitat, diet, its predators, how it raises its young, and more.

Safety Note

Nature can be unpredictable, so don't go outdoors alone, and always tell an adult when you're going outside. All wild animals should be treated with respect. If you see one—big or small—don't get close to it or attempt to touch or feed it. Instead, keep your distance and enjoy spotting it. If you can, snap some pictures with a camera or make a quick drawing using a sketchbook. If the animal is getting too close, is acting strangely, or seems sick or injured, tell an adult right away, as it might have rabies, a disease that can affect mammals. The good news is there's a rabies vaccine, so it's important to visit a doctor right away if you get bit or scratched by a wild animal.

Notes About Icons

Each species page includes basic information about each animal, from what it eats to how it survives the winter. The book also includes information that's neat to know; in the mammals section, each page includes a simple track illustration of each animal, with approximate track size included. And along the bottom, there is an example track pattern for each mammal, with the exception for those that primarily glide or fly (flying squirrels and bats).

On the left-hand page for each mammal, a rough-size illustration is included that shows how big each animal is compared to a basketball.

Also on the left-hand page, there are icons that tell you when each animal is most active: nocturnal (at night), diurnal (during the day), or crepuscular (at dawn/dusk), so you know when to look. If an animal has a "zzz" icon, it hibernates during the winter. Some animals hibernate every winter, and their internal processes (breathing and heartbeat) slow down almost entirely. Other animals only partially hibernate, but this still helps them save energy and survive through the coldest part of the year.

nocturnal
(active at night)

diurnal
(active during day)

crepuscular
(most active at
dawn and dusk)

hibernates/deep sleeper
(dormant during winter)

ground nest

cup nest

platform nest

cavity nest

migrates

On the left-hand side of each bird page, the nest for each species is shown, along with information on whether or not the bird migrates; on the right-hand side, there's information on where it goes.

Did you know?

Badgers are solitary animals, but they will sometimes hunt with coyotes in a team. A coyote will chase prey into the badger's den, and the badger will chase or dig out the prey that coyotes like. The badger's den has one entrance with a pile of dirt next to it. When a badger is threatened, it will back into its burrow and show its teeth.

Size Comparison Most Active Track Size Hibernates

   2¾"

American Badger

Taxidea taxus

Size: 2–3 feet long; weighs 8–25 pounds

Habitat: Savannas, grasslands, and meadows

Range: Can be found statewide in Iowa and westward through the Great Plains to the West Coast and southward to Mexico

Food: Carnivores, they eat pocket gophers, moles, ground squirrels, and other rodents. They will also eat dead animals (or carrion), fish, reptiles, and a few types of birds, especially ground-nesting birds.

Den: Badgers are fossorial (a digging animal that spends a lot of time underground); they build many dens or burrows throughout their range. Most dens are used to store food, but badgers also use dens to sleep in and raise their young. Dens can be over 10 feet deep and 4 feet wide.

Young: Cubs are born, with eyes closed, usually in April or May in litters of 2–3. Extensive care is provided by the mom for up to 3 months. After another 2–3 months, the young will gain their independence.

Predators: Bears, bobcats, mountain lions, coyotes, gray wolves, golden eagles, and humans

Tracks: The front tracks are 2¾ inches long and 2 inches wide.

The American badger is a short, bulky mammal with grayish to dirty-red fur. Badgers have a distinctive face with a series of cream-and-white stripes offset by a black background.

Did you know?

Beavers are rodents! Yes, these flat-tailed mammals are rodents, like rats and squirrels. In fact, they are the largest native rodents in North America. Just like other rodents, beavers have large incisors, which they use to chew through trees to build dams and dens. Beavers are the original wetland engineers. By damming rivers and streams, beavers create ponds and wetlands.

Size Comparison   Most Active   Track Size

6"

14

American Beaver

Castor canadensis

Size: Body is 25–30 inches long; tail is 9–13 inches long; weighs 30–70 pounds

Habitat: Wooded wetland areas near ponds, streams, and lakes

Range: Beavers can be found throughout Iowa and in much of the rest of the United States.

Food: Leaves, twigs, and stems; they also feed on fruits and aquatic plant roots; throughout the year they gather and store tree cuttings, which they eat in winter.

Den: A beaver's home is called a lodge. It consists of a pile of branches that is splattered with mud and vegetation. Lodges are constructed on the banks of lakes and streams and have exits and entrances that are underwater.

Young: Young beavers (kits) are born in late April through May and June in litters of 3–4. After two years they are considered mature and will be forced out of the den.

Predators: Bobcats, mountain lions, bears, wolves, and coyotes. Human trappers are major predators too.

Tracks: A beaver's front foot looks a lot like your hand; it has five fingers. The hind (back) foot is long, with five separate toes that have webbing or extra skin between them.

Beavers range from dark brown to reddish brown. They have a stocky body with hind legs that are longer than the front legs. The beaver's body is covered in dense fur, but its tail is naked and has special blood vessels that help it cool or warm its body.

Did you know?

American mink have webbed feet, like otters. Although they usually dive and swim short distances, mink can dive over 13 feet deep and swim for over 95 feet underwater, if necessary!

Size Comparison   Most Active   Track Size

1¾"

16

American Mink

Mustela vison

Size: 16–27 inches long; weighs 1½–3½ pounds

Habitat: Wetland areas with dense vegetation near streams, lakes, and swamps

Range: They are found throughout the state of Iowa, as well as most of the US and Canada.

Food: Fish, eggs, snakes, muskrats, farm animals, small mammals, and aquatic animals such as crayfish

Den: Their dens are near water, in holes in the ground, hollow logs, and old muskrat and beaver lodges; they will use grass or fur from prey as bedding.

Young: At birth, they weigh less than an ounce; mothers give birth to 3–6 young, called kits. They are mature at 1 year old.

Predators: Otters, birds of prey, wolves, coyotes, bobcats, internal parasites, and humans (who trap them for fur)

Tracks: Both the front and hind tracks resemble a gloved hand. Both the left and right tracks are seen parallel to each other because the mink often bound (leap) when moving. Tracks are usually seen near water.

A mostly nocturnal (active at night) animal, it has a shiny or glossy dark-brown coat that it keeps all year long. Mink usually have a white or pale-yellow chest patch or bib on the throat that sometimes extends to the belly.

Did you know?

It's a common misconception that bats are blind, but, in fact, they can see. However, they still rely on a special technique called echolocation to find food and to travel throughout the night sky. A female bat of reproductive age can eat her own body weight in insects in a single night. She does so while eating on the wing, meaning eating while in flight.

Size Comparison Most Active Hibernates

Big Brown Bat

Eptesicus fuscus

Size: 4–5 inches long; wingspan is 12–16 inches; weighs ½–1 ounce

Habitat: Cities, forests, deserts, mountains, and meadows

Range: Big brown bats are found statewide in Iowa. They can also be found in north-central areas of Canada, throughout the US into Mexico, Central America, and northern areas of South America.

Food: Insectivorous (insect eater); beetles make up most of their diet. They also feed on flies, wasps, and moths.

Den: Roosts in a nursing colony that may contain 40–100 or more pregnant females. Reproductive males, or bachelors, usually roost alone or in small groups. Bats roost in mines, tree cavities, under bridges and other manmade structures, and in rock crevices.

Young: Young bats (pups) are born blind, without fur, between May and June. Pups will feed on milk for approximately 4–5 weeks. They will start the process of learning to fly at around 3–5 weeks and become independent a couple of weeks later.

Predators: Snakes, owls, raccoons, feral cats, and humans

Tracks: Though they are rarely on the ground to leave a track, it would show as one thumbprint from the forearm and a hind footprint.

Big brown bats are large and have a furry back that's glossy brown to earthy red. They have a light-brown belly, hairless black wings, and rounded ears. In winter, they hibernate in tree cavities, manmade structures, and rock crevices. They maintain temperatures above 31 degrees and up to 42 degrees Fahrenheit.

The big brown bat does not often leave tracks.

Did you know?

Bobcats get their name from their short tail; a "bob" is a type of short haircut. They have the largest range of all wild cats in the United States. Bobcats can even hunt prey much larger than themselves; in fact, they can take down prey that is over four times their size, such as white-tailed deer!

Size Comparison   Most Active   Track Size

Bobcat

Lynx rufus

Size: 27–48 inches head to tail; males weigh around 30 pounds, while females weigh 24 pounds or so.

Habitat: Dense forests, scrub areas (forests of low trees and bushes), swamps, and even some urban (city) areas

Range: In Iowa, they can be found pretty much statewide, but sightings are rare in the central and northern quarters of the state; they are widespread throughout the United States.

Food: Squirrels, birds, rabbits, white-tailed jackrabbits, and white-tailed deer fawns; occasionally even adult deer!

Den: Dense shrubs, caves, or even hollow trees; dens can be lined with leaves or moss.

Young: Bobcats usually breed in early winter through spring. Females give birth to a litter of 2–4 kittens. Bobcats become independent around 7–8 months, and they reach reproductive maturity at 1 year for females and at 2 years for males.

Predators: Occasionally fishers and coyotes; humans also hunt and trap bobcats for fur.

Tracks: Roughly 2 inches wide; both front and back paws have four toe pads and a carpal pad (a pad below the toe pads).

Bobcats have a white belly and a brown or pale-gray top with black spots. The tail usually has a black tip. They are mostly crepuscular (say it, cre-pus-cue-lar), which means they are most active in the dawn and twilight hours.

Did you know?
At one time, coyotes were only found in the central and western parts of the US, but now, with the help of humans (eliminating predators and clearing forests), they can be found throughout most of the country. Coyotes can jump over 3 meters horizontally.

Size Comparison   Most Active   Track Size

2"

22

Coyote

Canis latrans

Size: 3–4 feet long; weighs 21–50 pounds

Habitat: Urban and suburban areas, woodlands, grasslands, and farm fields

Range: Coyotes can be found statewide in Iowa. They are also found throughout the US and Mexico, the northern parts of Central America, and in southern Canada.

Food: A variety of prey, including rodents, birds, deer, and sometimes livestock

Den: Coyotes will dig their own dens but will often use old fox or badger dens or hollow logs.

Young: 5–7 pups, independent around 8–10 months

Predators: Bears and wolves; humans trap and kill for pelts and to "protect" livestock.

Tracks: Four toes and a carpal pad (the single pad below the toe pads) can be seen on all four feet.

Coyotes have brown, reddish-brown, or gray back fur with a lighter gray-to-white belly. They have a longer muzzle than other wild canines. They are active mostly during the night (nocturnal) but also during the twilight and dawn hours (crepuscular).

Did you know?

Chipmunks get their English name from the "chip" or alert calls they use when they sense a threat. Eastern chipmunks are not fully herbivores (plant eaters); in fact, they eat a variety of things, including other mammals and amphibians, like frogs.

Size Comparison   Most Active   Track Size   Hibernates

¾"

Eastern Chipmunk

Tamias striatus

Size: Body is 3–6 inches long; tail is 3–4 inches long; weighs 2½–5½ ounces

Habitat: Suburban areas, woodlands, and dense scrub areas

Range: They can be found in much of Iowa, throughout the eastern US, and in southern Canada.

Food: Berries, nuts, seeds, frogs, insects

Den: Has multiple chambers (or rooms); the entrance is usually hidden under brush, fallen trees, rock piles, and human-made landscaping items.

Young: 2–8 young (kits) per litter, 2 litters per year. Born blind and without fur. Weigh under an ounce at birth. Eyes open at 4 weeks, becomes independent at 8 weeks

Predators: Coyotes, feral and outdoor house cats, snakes, weasels, bobcats, hawks, and owls

Tracks: The front foot has four digit (toe) pads and is ½ inch long; the hind foot has five digit pads and is just under ¾ inch.

Chipmunks are small rodents with brown base colors, seven alternating stripes, and white bellies. During winter, they will stay underground. They hide food in underground caches that they will feed on through the winter.

Did you know?

The eastern cottontail gets its name from its short, puffy tail that looks like a cotton ball. A cottontail can travel up to 18 miles per hour! Rabbits have great hearing and eyesight. They can almost see all the way around them (360 degrees). On days with high wind, they will bed down in a burrow because the wind interferes with their ability to hear and detect predators.

Size Comparison   Most Active   Track Size

3½"

Eastern Cottontail

Sylvilagus floridanus

Size: 16–19 inches long; weighs 1½–4 pounds

Habitat: Forests, swamps, orchards, deserts, and farm areas

Range: Found statewide in Iowa; throughout the eastern US to Arizona and New Mexico; isolated ranges in the Pacific Northwest

Food: Clovers; grasses; wild strawberries; garden plants; and twigs of a variety of trees, including maple, oak, and sumac

Den: Rabbits don't dig dens; they bed in shallow, grassy, saucer-shaped depressions (holes) or under shrubs. They will sometimes use woodchuck dens in the winter.

Young: They usually have 2–4 kits at one time, but it's not uncommon to have 7 or more. Born naked and blind, they weigh about an ounce (about the same weight as a slice of bread) and gain weight very quickly.

Predators: Owls, coyotes, eagles, weasels, humans, and foxes

Tracks: The front foot is an inch long with four toe pads; the hind foot is 3½ inches long.

An eastern cottontail sports thick brown fur with a white belly, a gray rump, and a white "cotton" tail. During the winter, it survives by eating bark off of fruit trees and shrubs.

Did you know?

The eastern fox squirrel's bones appear pink under ultraviolet (UV) light, a type of light human eyes can't see. Squirrels accidentally help plant trees by forgetting where they have previously buried nuts. Sometimes, they seem to pretend to bury nuts to throw off would-be nut thieves.

Size Comparison   Most Active   Track Size

2½"

Eastern Fox Squirrel

Sciurus niger

Size: 19–28 inches long; weighs 1–3 pounds

Habitat: Open woodlands, suburban areas, and dense forests

Range: They are common statewide in Iowa and the eastern United States; they are found as far south as Texas and as far north as the Dakotas.

Food: Acorns, seeds, nuts, insects such as moths and beetles, birds, eggs, and dead fish

Den: Ball-shaped dreys, or nests, are made of vegetation like leaves, sometimes in tree cavities.

Young: 2–3 kits are born between late January to April and late June through August. Kittens are born naked and weigh half an ounce; they are cared for by their parents for the first 7–8 weeks. They can reproduce by around 10–11 months for males and 8 months for females.

Predators: Humans, hawks, cats, coyotes, bobcats, and weasels

Tracks: The front tracks have four digits (toes), and the hind feet have five digits.

The eastern fox squirrel is the largest tree squirrel in Massachusetts. It is gray or reddish brown with a yellowish or light-brown underside. There is also a rare black and smoky-gray phases. Both the male and female look the same.

Did you know?

Weasels are small but tough! They will attack prey over three times their own size, and they help control rodent and pest species by eating mice, voles, and other small mammals.

Size Comparison   Most Active   Track Size

1¾"

Long-tailed weasel

Mustela frenata

Size: 14–18 inches long; weighs 5 ounces to 1 pound

Habitat: Forests, farms, and rocky areas

Range: Weasels can be found statewide in Iowa and the rest of the United States, except for a small pocket in southern California, Nevada, and Arizona.

Food: Ducks and other birds, frogs, rodents, rabbits, and sometimes domesticated chickens and eggs; they will hide extra food to eat later.

Den: Weasels will dig dens but will also use rock piles, abandoned burrows of other animals, or hollow logs. Dens are covered with fur and grass.

Young: 4–8 kits are born in April; they reach adult weight within 4 months.

Predators: Hawks, owls, coyotes, foxes, humans, and cats

Tracks: The front foot is wider than the hind foot. Each foot has five toe pads with four claws extending from them.

Long-tailed weasels have several color phases, including alternating from brown to white as the seasons change from summer to winter.

Did you know?

Muskrats are well adapted for the aquatic (water) environment they live in; they can hold their breath for over 10 minutes, and they can swim backwards! Their fur also helps them float and move through the water.

Size Comparison   Most Active   Track Size

Muskrat

Ondatra zibethicus

Size: 8–13 inches long; tail is 6½–12 inches long; weighs 2–4 pounds

Habitat: Marshes, streams, ponds, and lakes

Range: They can be found statewide in Iowa, as well as in most of the US, except in deep southern areas like parts of Florida, Texas, California, and a few other Southwestern states.

Food: Crayfish, snails, frogs, and aquatic plants such as water lilies and cattails

Den: Like beavers, muskrats are builders. They build lodges that are 2 feet high and 4 feet across; these can be used for multiple generations and are found near the water's edge.

Young: Muskrats can have 2 or more litters (groups of babies) a year. They usually give birth to 6–8 muskrats that weigh around an ounce and are blind at birth. Baby muskrats open their eyes at around 15 days and nurse (drink milk from the mother) for 4 weeks.

Predators: Foxes, raccoons, coyotes, mink, eagles, hawks, and owls

Tracks: They have pads with four toes on the front and five toes on the hind feet. The hind feet have webbing.

Muskrats have brown-to-reddish fur with a grayish belly and a long tail. In winter, muskrats gnaw holes in the ice and push vegetation through them. These are called pushups and are used as feeding sites.

Did you know?

The raccoon is great at catching fish and other aquatic animals, such as mussels and crayfish. They are also excellent swimmers, but they apparently avoid swimming because the water makes their fur heavy. Raccoons can turn their feet 180 degrees; this helps them when climbing, especially when going headfirst down trees.

Size Comparison	Most Active	Track Size	Hibernates
		3"	

Northern Raccoon

Procyon lotor

Size: 24–40 inches long; weighs 15–28 pounds

Habitat: Woody areas, grasslands, suburban and urban areas, wetlands, and marshes

Range: They are found throughout Iowa and the US; they are also found in Mexico and southern Canada.

Food: Eggs, insects, garbage, garden plants, berries, nuts, fish, carrion, small mammals, and aquatic invertebrates like crayfish and mussels

Den: Raccoon dens are built in hollow trees, abandoned burrows, caves, and human-made structures.

Young: 2–6 young (kits) are born around March through July. They are born weighing 2 ounces, are around 4 inches long, and are blind with lightly colored fur.

Predators: Coyotes, foxes, bobcats, humans, and even large birds of prey

Tracks: Their front tracks resemble human handprints. The back tracks sort of look like human footprints.

The northern raccoon has dense fur with variations of brown, black, and white streaks. It has black, mask-like markings on its face and a black-and-gray/brownish ringed tail. During the fall, it will grow a thick layer of fat to stay warm in the winter.

Did you know?

Otters are good swimmers and can close their nostrils while diving. This allows them to dive for as long as 8 minutes and to depths of over 50 feet. Otter fur is the thickest of all mammal fur. River otters have an incredible 67,000 hairs for every square centimeter!

Size Comparison   Most Active   Track Size

3"

Northern River Otter

Lontra canadensis

Size: 29–48 inches long; weighs 10–33 pounds

Habitat: Lakes, marshes, rivers, and large streams; suburban areas

Range: Otters can be found statewide in Iowa; they are found across much of the US, except parts of the Southwest and portions of the central US.

Food: Fish, frogs, snakes, crabs, crayfish, mussels, birds, eggs, turtles, and small mammals. They sometimes eat aquatic vegetation too.

Den: They den in burrows along the river, usually under rocks, riverbanks, hollow trees, and vegetation.

Young: 2–4 young (pups) are born between November and May. Pups are born with their eyes closed. They will leave the area at around 6 months old and reach full maturity at around 2 or 3 years.

Predators: Coyotes, bobcats, bears, and dogs

Tracks: Their feet have nonretractable claws and are webbed.

Northern river otters have thick, dark-brown fur with a long, slender body. Their fur is made up of two types: a short undercoat and a coarse top coat that repels water. They have webbed feet and a layer of fat that helps keep them warm in cold water.

Did you know?

The red fox is a great jumper and can leap over 13 feet in one bound. Red foxes are also fast, as they can run up to 30 miles per hour. Red foxes, like wild cats, will hide their food to eat later, often under leaf litter or in holes.

Size Comparison   Most Active   Track Size

2¼"

Red Fox
Vulpes vulpes

Size: 37–42 inches long; weighs 8–15 pounds

Habitat: Grasslands, forest edges, farm fields, and suburban areas

Range: Foxes can be seen throughout much of Iowa; they can be found in nearly all of the US, except for the Southwest.

Food: They are omnivores that eat frogs, birds, snakes, small mammals, insects, seeds, nuts, and fruit.

Den: They dig underground dens, sometimes several at once, splitting a litter (babies) between the two. They also use old badger or groundhog holes or tree roots for den sites.

Young: 3–7 young (kits) are born; pups will nurse (drink milk from the mother) for around 10 weeks and will become independent at around 7 months.

Predators: Coyotes, lynx, cougars, and other species of carnivores. Humans trap and hunt foxes for fur.

Tracks: Their footprints resemble dog tracks and have four toe pads; they walk in a line with the hind foot behind the front.

The red fox is a medium-size predator with a burnt orange or rust-like red coat with a bushy, white-tipped tail. The legs are usually black or grayish. The red fox's tail is about one third of its body length.

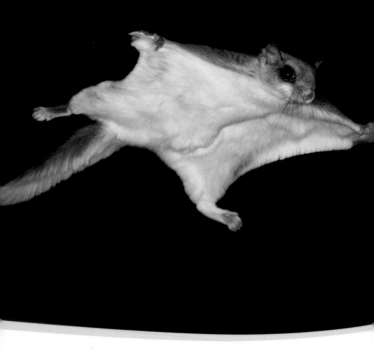

Did you know?

The southern flying squirrel doesn't actually fly! Instead, it uses special folds of skin to glide through the air. They can glide over 100 feet at a time. They have thick paws that aid them in landing. Because they move from tree to tree, they help to spread seeds and fungi.

Size Comparison   Most Active

Southern Flying Squirrel

Glaucomys volans

Size: 9 inches long; weighs 2–3 ounces

Habitat: Forests with older trees

Range: They can be found throughout much of Iowa, except in the western corner of the state; throughout the eastern US; and in parts of Mexico.

Food: Nuts, berries, acorns, small birds, mice, insects, and mushrooms

Den: They make nests in tree hollows. They will also use abandoned woodpecker holes and human-made nest boxes or birdhouses. They line the nest with chewed bark, grasses, moss, and feathers.

Young: 2–3 young (kits) are born per litter; they drink milk from the mother for around 70 days and will be fully independent around 4 months and mature at around a year old.

Predators: Small hawks, foxes, owls, martens (weasel-like mammals), and weasels

Tracks: Tracks are rare because they spend most of their time in trees.

The southern flying squirrel is a grayish-brown nocturnal (active at night) animal that glides through the air from tree to tree. The patagium, or skin fold, stretches from their ankles to their wrist, allowing them to "fly." (People have even built similar "squirrel suits" to glide with, and they've worked!) During winter months, flying squirrels share cavities with others.

The southern flying squirrel does not often leave tracks.

Did you know?

Skunks help farmers! They save farmers money by feeding on rodents and insects that destroy crops. When skunks spray, they can aim really well! When threatened, a skunk will aim its tail towards the threat and spray a stinky musk into the target's face or eyes.

Size Comparison   Most Active   Track Size 1½"   Hibernates

Striped Skunk

Mephitis mephitis

Size: 17–30 inches long; weighs 6–13 pounds

Habitat: Woodlands, prairies, and suburban areas

Range: Found statewide in Iowa; they can be found throughout the US and into Canada and the northern parts of Mexico.

Food: Omnivores (eaters of meat and plants), they eat eggs, fruits, nuts, small mammals, carrion (dead things), insects, amphibians, small reptiles, and even garbage.

Den: Skunks prefer short and shallow natural dens, or dens abandoned by other animals, but will dig dens 3–6 feet long and up to 3 feet deep underground. Dens have multiple hidden entrances, and rooms are usually lined with vegetation.

Young: They have 4–5 young (kits) that are blind at birth; at around 3 weeks they gain vision and the ability to spray.

Predators: Raptors and large carnivores

Tracks: Their front feet have five long, curved claws used for digging; the hind foot also has five toes and is longer and skinnier than the front foot.

The striped skunk is a cat-size, nocturnal (active at night) mammal with black fur and two white stripes that run the entire length of the body. The stripe pattern is usually distinctive to each skunk.

Did you know?
As their name suggests, these squirrels have 13 lines on their back; the darker brown lines are wider than the lighter tan lines. These ground squirrels will greet each other by touching noses or lips.

Size Comparison   Most Active   Track Size   Hibernates

        1¼"

Thirteen-lined Ground Squirrel

Ictidomys tridecemlineatus

Size: 9½–11 inches long; weighs 5–9 ounces

Habitat: Beaches and sandy areas, grasslands, meadows, and farm fields

Range: They are found throughout the state of Iowa; they are also found from the north-central US south into New Mexico.

Food: Seeds, fruits, grasses, flowers, insects, reptiles, and small birds

Den: Gophers build burrows underground.

Young: They have a litter of 6–8 (young) kits that are born blind, naked, and without teeth. Their stripes start to show up after 10 days. Kits become adults at around 9 months.

Predators: Hawks, owls, coyotes, weasels, snakes, and foxes

Tracks: Each front foot has four digits (toes); the hind foot has five digits and is longer than the front foot.

The thirteen-lined ground squirrel is golden to light brown with 13 alternating lines of dark brown and tan along its back with a light pale-to-white belly or underbody. The thirteen-lined ground squirrel will hibernate during the winter.

Did you know?

Tricolored bats got their name because of the three different colors of fur on their back: dark gray on the bottom, golden-brown in the middle, and brown or earth-tone red on the top. The tricolored bat is the smallest bat in Iowa!

Size Comparison   Most Active   Hibernates

Tricolored Bat
Perimyotis subflavus

Size: 3–3½ inches long; wingspan is 8⅓–10⅓ inches; weighs ⅒–¾ ounce or about as much as a quarter

Habitat: Forests, caves, urban (city) areas, grasslands, and orchards

Range: Widespread across the eastern and central US as far west as Texas, it can be found throughout Iowa.

Food: Mosquitoes, beetles, ants, moths, and cicadas

Den: Roost in trees, buildings, culverts (sewage drains), caves, and in Spanish moss. Females will roost in colonies of 25 or more individuals. Males are solitary and do not have bachelor colonies like other bat species. Bats mate in the fall and give birth in the spring.

Young: Pups are born blind and furless in June and July. Pups learn to fly 3 weeks after birth, and within a month they are able to hunt for themselves. They are mature by their first fall but will not usually mate until their second fall.

Predators: Owls, raccoons, snakes, and hawks

Tracks: Though they are rarely on the ground to leave a track, it would show as one thumbprint from the forearm and a hind footprint.

Tricolored bats are a golden hue of yellowish and brown fur. Single hairs are darkly shaded at the bottom, yellow hued in the midsection, and brown at the tip. This is the reason for the name "tricolored." During the winter they hibernate in caves, mines, and rock crevices. In areas with a lack of caves or mines, they hibernate in roadside culverts.

The tricolored bat does not often leave tracks.

Did you know?

The opossum is the only marsupial native to the US. Marsupials are a special group of animals that are most well-known for their pouches, which they use to carry their young. When frightened, young opossums will play dead (called playing possum) and adults will show their teeth and hiss or run away.

Size Comparison   Most Active   Track Size

2½"

Virginia Opossum

Didelphis virginiana

Size: 22–45 inches long; weighs 4–8 pounds

Habitat: Forests, woodlands, meadows, and suburban areas

Range: They are found statewide in Iowa; they are found throughout the eastern US, Canada, and also in Mexico and Costa Rica.

Food: Eggs, small mammals, garbage, insects, worms, birds, fruit, and occasionally small reptiles and amphibians

Den: They den in hollow trees, abandoned animal burrows, and buildings.

Young: A litter of 6–20 young (joeys) are born blind and without fur; their limbs are not fully formed. Young will climb from the birthing area into the mother's pouch and stay until 8 weeks old; they then alternate between the mother's pouch and her back for 4 weeks. At 12 weeks they are independent.

Predators: Hawks, owls, pet cats and dogs, coyotes, and bobcats

Tracks: The front feet are 2 inches long and around 1½ inches wide and resemble a child's hands; the hind feet are 2½ inches long and around 2¼ inches wide; they have fingers in front with a fifth finger that acts as a thumb.

The Virginia opossum has long gray-and-black fur; the face is white, and the tail is pink to gray and furless. Opossums have long claws.

Did you know?

When they first emerge, a deer's antlers are covered in a special skin called velvet. Deer can run up to 40 miles per hour and can jump over 8 feet vertically (high) and over 15 feet horizontally (long).

Size Comparison

Most Active

Track Size

White-tailed Deer

Odocoileus virginianus

Size: 4–6 feet long; 3–4 feet tall at front shoulder; weighs 114–308 pounds

Habitat: Forest edges, brushy fields, woody farmlands, prairies, and swamps

Range: They are found statewide in Iowa and throughout the US, except for much of the Southwest; they are also found in southern Canada and into South America.

Food: Fruits, grasses, tree shrubs, nuts, and bark

Den: Deer do not den but will bed down in tall grasses and shrubby areas.

Young: Deer usually give birth to twins (fawns) that are 3–6 pounds in late May to June. The fawns are born with spots; this coloration helps them hide in vegetation. Young become independent at 1–2 years.

Predators: Wolves, coyotes, bears, bobcats, and humans

Tracks: Both front and hind feet have two teardrop- or comma-shaped toes.

Crepuscular (active at dawn and dusk), white-tailed deer have big brown eyes with eye rings and a long snout with a black, glossy nose. The males have antlers, which fall off each year. All deer have a white tail that they flash upward when alarmed. Deer molt or change fur color twice a year. They sport a rusty-brown fur in the summer; in early fall, they transition to winter coats that are grayish brown in color.

Did you know?

White-tailed jackrabbits are hares, not rabbits. The difference is that rabbits are born without fur and are smaller, while hares are larger and born with fur. Jackrabbits have powerful legs that allow them to reach speeds over 35 miles per hour and leap more than 10 feet.

Size Comparison   Most Active   Track Size

2½—5½"

White-tailed Jackrabbit

Lepus townsendii

Size: 2 feet long; weighs 3–9 pounds

Habitat: Mountainous slopes, alpine tundra, sagebrush, prairies, meadows, and farm fields

Range: They can be found in Canada and the western US from Washington into California and as far east as Wisconsin and Illinois. In Iowa, they can be found statewide but are rarely seen.

Food: Jackrabbits are herbivores that mainly eat plants like alfalfa and clover. In the fall and winter months, they will also eat woody vegetation.

Den: No den; bunnies are born in hollow depressions.

Young: Bunnies are born (after a 40-day pregnancy) covered with fur and are active soon after birth. Young nurse for only a few days and reach reproductive maturity within their first year.

Predators: Coyotes, foxes, raptors (birds of prey), bobcats, badgers, and weasels

Tracks: Front feet are around 2–2½ inches long and 1¼–1¾ inches wide. Hind feet are 2½–5½ inches long and around 1½–2½ inches wide.

The white-tailed jackrabbit is a large, long-eared hare. It has grayish-brown-to-yellowish-brown fur with a paler underside and black-tipped ears. The white-tailed jackrabbit has very long front and rear legs. It has a white tail and is bigger than the black-tailed jackrabbit. Males and females look alike, but females are usually larger.

Did you know?

Woodchucks are important parts of the ecosystem. Their abandoned burrows are used by several other types of wildlife, including foxes, weasels, skunks, and possums. "Whistle-pig" is another common name for woodchucks; this is because they make a high-pitched whistle sound when alarmed, alerting nearby groundhogs of danger.

Size Comparison	Most Active	Track Size	Hibernates

Woodchuck (Groundhog)

Marmota monax

Size: 21½–30 inches long; weighs 6–11 pounds

Habitat: Forest edges, rocky areas, and meadows

Range: They are found statewide in Iowa, as well as in much of the eastern US and into parts of the South.

Food: Wild grasses, berries, insects, and farm crops; groundhogs also feast on gardens.

Den: They build summer and winter dens that have multiple entrances.

Young: 4–6 kits are born in late April to early May; groundhogs are independent at 2 months and adults at 1 year old.

Predators: Red foxes, coyotes, black bears, snakes, hawks, and bobcats

Tracks: The front feet are 1¾ inches long, with four digits resembling fingers; the hind feet are 2 inches long with five digits.

A woodchuck is a large brown rodent that has two layers of waterproof fur. This fur helps them to stay warm in the winter and helps them dry quickly after being in the water. Groundhogs eat a lot of food in the summer and survive the winter by using the excess fat they build up.

Did you know?

The American goldfinch helps restore habitats by spreading seeds. The goldfinch gets its color from a pigment called a carotenoid (say it, cuh-rot-en-oid) in the seeds it eats. It can even feed upside down by using its feet to bring seeds to its mouth.

Nest Type   Most Active

American Goldfinch

Spinus tristis

Size: 4½–5 inches long; wingspan of 9 inches; weighs about half an ounce

Habitat: Grasslands, meadows, suburban areas, and wetlands

Range: Found throughout Iowa year-round; they can be found throughout much of the United States and southern Canada during various times of the year.

Food: Seeds of plants and trees; sometimes feeds on insects; loves thistle seeds at birdfeeders

Nesting: Goldfinches build a nest in late June.

Nest: Cup-shaped nests are built a couple of feet above-ground out of roots and plant fibers.

Eggs: 2–7 eggs with a bluish-white tint

Young: Young (chicks) hatch around 15 days after being laid; they hatch without feathers and weigh only a gram. Chicks learn to fly after around 11–15 days. Young become mature at around 11 months old.

Predators: Garter snakes, blue jays, American kestrels, and cats

Migration: Nonmigratory in Iowa; in some states, it will migrate north for breeding territories and south for wintering areas.

During the summer, American goldfinch males are brightly colored with golden-yellow feathers and an orange beak. They have black wings with white wing bars. The crown (top) of the head is black. In winter, they molt, and the males look more like the females. Females are always greenish yellow with hints of yellow around the head.

Did you know?

American robins have a great sense of hearing. They hunt for earthworms underground using only their hearing. Robins are opportunistic feeders in urban (city) areas; they will wait for lawns to be disturbed by mowers, sprinklers, or rain, and then feed on the worms that have emerged.

Nest Type   Most Active

American Robin

Turdus migratorius

Size: 9–11 inches long; wingspan of 17 inches; weighs 2½–3 ounces

Habitat: Cities, forests, and lawns

Range: They can be found throughout Iowa year-round; during the breeding season, they can be found throughout North America, except for the extreme north of Canada.

Food: Fruits, earthworms, beetle grubs, caterpillars, insects, and grasshoppers

Nesting: April to August

Nest: Cup-shaped nests are exclusively built by the female 5–14 feet off the ground in bushes or trees. Nests are constructed of grass, paper, twigs, and feathers. A new nest is built for each set of eggs.

Eggs: 3–5 sky-blue eggs

Young: Eggs hatch after 14 days of incubation; chicks hatch blind and mostly without feathers. Hatchlings (chicks) leave the nest after 2 weeks but will continue to beg for food from parents.

Predators: Snakes, crows, cats, foxes, raccoons, squirrels, raptors, and weasels

Migration: They do not migrate.

American robin males have a dark black-to-gray head with a yellow bill, a brown back, a rusty-orange chest, and a whitish ring around the eyes. Females are similar in color but are not as bright as males, and they usually have a brownish head.

Did you know?

The bald eagle is an endangered species success story! The bald eagle was once endangered due to a pesticide called DDT that weakened eggshells and caused them to crack early. Through the banning of DDT and other conservation efforts, the bald eagle population recovered, and it was removed from the Endangered Species List in July of 2007.

Nest Type

Most Active

Migrates

Bald Eagle

Haliaeetus leucocephalus

Size: 3½ feet long; wingspan of 6½–8 feet; weighs 8–14 pounds

Habitat: Forests and tree stands (small forests) near river edges, lakes, seashores, and wetlands

Range: In Iowa, they are mostly nonbreeding residents, with a small area of eastern Iowa hosting year-round residents. They are found throughout much of the US.

Food: Fish, waterfowl (ducks), rabbits, squirrels, muskrats, and deer carcasses; will steal food from other eagles or ospreys

Nesting: Eagles have lifelong partners that begin nesting in fall, laying eggs November–February.

Nest: They build a large nest out of sticks, high up in trees; the nest can be over 5 feet wide and over 6 feet tall, often shaped like an upside-down cone.

Eggs: 1–3 white eggs

Young: Young (chicks) will hatch at around 35 days; young will leave the nest at around 12 weeks. It takes up to 5 years for eagles to get that iconic look!

Predators: Few; collisions with cars sometimes occur.

Migration: Migrate north during the spring for breeding, and back south in the fall to nonbreeding grounds

Adult bald eagles have a dark-brown body, a white head and tail, and a golden-yellow beak. Juvenile eagles are mostly brown at first, but their color pattern changes over their first few years. A bald eagle can use its wings as oars to propel itself across bodies of water.

Did you know?
The barred owl has dark-brown eyes; many other owls have yellow eyes. Barred owls, like other owls, have special structures on their primary feathers that allow them to fly silently through the air.

Nest Type   Most Active

Barred Owl

Strix varia

Size: 17–20 inches long; wingspan of 3½ feet; weighs 2 pounds

Habitat: Forested areas, near floodplains of lakes and rivers

Range: They are year-round residents in Iowa; they are found throughout the eastern US and southern Canada, with scattered populations throughout the Pacific Northwest.

Food: Squirrels, rabbits, and mice; will also prey on birds and aquatic animals like frogs, fish, and crayfish

Nesting: Courtship starts in late fall; nesting starts in winter.

Nest: They use hollow trees; they will also use abandoned nests of other animals and human-made nest structures.

Eggs: 2–4 white eggs with a rough shell

Young: Young (chicks) hatch between 27 and 33 days; they have white down feathers and leave the nest around 5 weeks after hatching. They are fully independent at around 6 months and fully mature at around 2 years.

Predators: Great horned owls, raccoons, weasels, and sometimes northern goshawks feed on eggs and young in the nest.

Migration: Barred owls do not migrate.

The barred owl is a medium-size bird with dark rings highlighting the face. Their feathers are brown and grayish, often with streaking or a bar-like pattern. They have no ear tufts and have a rounded head with a yellow beak and brown eyes. They can easily be identified by their call: "Who cooks for you, who cooks for you all?"

Did you know?

Kingfishers inspired human technology! Bullet trains around the world are designed after the kingfisher's beak, which allows it to dive into water without a splash. This design was used in bullet trains to allow them to enter into tunnels without making a large booming sound. This process of modeling human technology after animal features is called biomimicry.

Nest Type   Most Active

Belted Kingfisher

Megaceryle alcyon

Size: 11–13¾ inches long; wingspan is 19–24 inches; weighs 5–6 ounces

Habitat: Forests and grassland areas near rivers, ponds, lakes

Range: Mostly year-round resident that can be found throughout Iowa as well as most of the United States and Canada

Food: Carnivores, they eat mostly fish and other aquatic animals, such as crayfish and frogs, and occasionally other birds, mammals, and berries.

Nesting: Nests are in the form of upward-sloped burrows that are dug in soft banks on or near water. (The upward slopes prevent flooding.)

Nest: Females and males select the nest site together; males do most of the digging.

Eggs: 5–8 white, smooth, glossy eggs are laid per clutch (group of eggs).

Young: Chicks are born featherless with pink skin, closed eyes, and a dark bill. They receive care from both parents. Chicks leave the nest after about 28 days.

Predators: Snakes, hawks, and mammals

Migration: They do not migrate.

The belted kingfisher is bluish gray on top; the bottom half is white with a blue/gray belt or band. The wings have white spots on them. Unlike most other birds, the kingfisher female has a different pattern than the male. Females have a second reddish-brown or rusty-orange band on their belly.

Did you know?

Black-capped chickadees have a unique strategy for surviving winter. The area of the brain that aids in memory (the hippocampus) temporarily gets bigger in preparation for winter. This allows them to remember where they hid or cached seeds.

Nest Type   Most Active

Black-capped Chickadee

Poecile atricapillus

Size: 5½–7½ inches long; wingspan of 8 inches; weighs about half an ounce

Habitat: Forests, woodland edges, and suburban and urban areas

Range: They are year-round residents of Iowa and can be found in the northern United States.

Food: Caterpillars, insects, seeds, spiders, and berries

Nesting: March to August

Nest: Chickadees utilize old woodpecker holes or make their own cup-shaped nests in tree cavities that have been weakened by rot.

Eggs: 4–6 eggs that are white with brown spots

Young: Eggs hatch 12–13 days after they are laid; chicks leave the nest around 15 days after hatching; chickadee parents continue feeding the young for another 5–6 weeks.

Predators: Hawks, owls, shrikes, raccoons, house cats left outside, and other mammals

Migration: They do not migrate.

A black-capped chickadee has a gray body with a black cap, or top of head, and a black throat and beak; they have white cheeks and light bellies.

Did you know?

Blue jays get the name "jay" from their noisy and rambunctious personality. Blue jays can mimic; they have been known to copy human speech and often fool birders by mimicking hawks. Sometimes blue jays will mimic hawk calls to scare birds into dropping food. Other possible explanations include using the call to warn other birds that a hawk may be nearby.

Nest Type   Most Active

Blue Jay

Cyanocitta cristata

Size: 11–12½ inches long; wingspan of 16 inches; weighs 2½–3½ ounces

Habitat: Forests and forest edges, suburban areas, city parks, and farm fields

Range: They are year-round residents in Iowa; their range extends from northeastern and central Canada and well into the West and the Great Plains.

Food: Acorns, seeds, insects, fruits, eggs, nuts, and carrion (dead animals)

Nesting: March to July

Nest: The gathering of nesting materials and the building of nests are shared by both male and female; a cup-shaped nest is built in the fork of tree branches.

Eggs: 4–5 eggs that are either blue or light brown and speckled with brown spots

Young: Chicks hatch naked with eyes closed around 17 days after eggs are laid. Nestlings are cared for by both parents and usually leave the nest 17–20 days after hatching.

Predators: Snakes, crows, falcons, owls, cats, raccoons, and hawks

Migration: Year-round residents that do not migrate

The blue jay's feathers appear blue, but they are actually brown. They look blue because of refraction, or the bending of light. It has a blue crest (feathers on its head); the underbody is white or gray. A blue jay can hold food items with its feet and use its beak to open them. Sometimes they will store food for later.

Did you know?

Blue-winged teals are the second-most abundant duck in North America! (The first is the mallard.) They are often one of the first ducks to migrate south during the fall and one of the last ones to return north each spring. Blue-winged teals get their name from the blue patch on their wings.

Nest Type

Most Active

Migrates

Blue-winged Teal

Spatula discors

Size: 16 inches long; wingspan of 23 inches; weighs 13 ounces

Habitat: Coastal areas, ponds, lakes, marshes, shallow streams, and prairies

Range: They can be found throughout most of North America. In Iowa, they are found statewide during the breeding season.

Food: They are omnivores that eat aquatic insects, snails, plants, and seeds.

Nesting: Mid-April to mid-May

Nest: Nests are built on the ground in grassy areas.

Eggs: They lay one clutch of about 6–13 creamy-white eggs.

Young: Ducklings hatch about a month after laying, covered in yellow down feathers. They can walk to water within several hours. They will fledge the nest within 40 days and reach reproductive maturity the first winter after hatching.

Predators: Long-tailed weasels, birds of prey, foxes, raccoons, and skunks

Migration: Migrate at night to and from breeding grounds in the fall and spring

Blue-winged teals are small ducks. They have a dusky-blue patch on their wings and large black bills. The male has a bluish-gray head with a white line between the eyes and bill. It has black spots on a gray breast, tan sides, and a rump that has a white patch on either side. Females are smaller and also have a dusty-blue patch on their wings. They are a duller brown compared to males. They both have yellow legs.

Did you know?

The great blue heron is the largest and most common heron species in Iowa. A heron's eye color changes as it ages. The eyes start out gray but transition to yellow over time. Great blue herons swallow prey whole.

Nest Type   Most Active

Great Blue Heron

Ardea herodias

Size: 3–4½ feet long; wingspan of 6–7 feet; weighs 5–7 pounds

Habitat: Lakes, ponds, rivers, marshes, lagoons, wetlands, and coastal areas like beaches

Range: They are year-round residents in Iowa; they can be found throughout the entirety of the United States and down into Mexico.

Food: Fish, rats, crabs, shrimp, grasshoppers, crayfish, other birds, small mammals, snakes, and lizards

Nesting: May to August

Nest: 2–3 feet across and saucer shaped; often grouped in large rookeries (colonies) in tall trees along the water's edge. Nests are built out of sticks and are often located in dead trees more than 100 feet above the ground; nests are used year after year.

Eggs: 3–7 pale bluish eggs

Young: Chicks will hatch after 28 days of incubation; young will stay in the nest for around 10 weeks. They reach reproductive maturity at just under 2 years.

Predators: Eagles, crows, gulls, raccoons, bears, and hawks

Migration: Does not migrate

The great blue heron is a large wading bird with blue and gray upper body feathers; the belly area is white. They have long yellow legs that they use to stalk prey in the water. Great blue herons are famous for stalking prey at the water's edge; their specially adapted feet keep them from sinking into the mud!

73

Did you know?

A great horned owl can exert a crushing force of over 300 pounds with its talons. Despite its name, the great horned owl doesn't have horns at all. Instead, the obvious tufts on its head are made of feathers. Scientists aren't sure exactly how the tufts function, but they may help them stay hidden.

Nest Type

Most Active

Great Horned Owl

Bubo virginianus

Size: Up to 23 inches long; wingspan of 45 inches; weighs 3 pounds

Habitat: Woods; swamps; desert edges; as well as heavily populated areas such as cities, suburbs, and parks

Range: In Iowa, they are year-round residents. They are found throughout the continent of North America.

Food: They eat a variety of foods, but mostly mammals. Sometimes they eat other birds as well.

Nesting: They have lifelong partnerships, with nesting season starting in early winter; egg-laying starts in mid-January to February.

Nest: Nests are found 20–50 feet off the ground. They tend to reuse nests from other raptors or hollowed-out trees.

Eggs: The female lays 2–4 whitish eggs. Eggs are incubated for around 30 days.

Young: Young can fly at around 9 weeks old. The parents care for and feed young for several months.

Predators: Young owls are preyed upon by foxes, coyotes, bears, and opossums. As adults, they are rarely attacked by other birds of prey, such as golden eagles and goshawks.

Migration: They do not migrate.

They are bulky birds with large ear tufts, a rusty brown-to-grayish face with a black border, and large bright eyes. The body color tends to be brown; the wing pattern is checkered with an intermingled dark brown. The chest and belly areas are light brown and have white bars.

75

Did you know?

Downy woodpeckers are the smallest woodpecker species in North America. Hairy woodpeckers can hear insects traveling under the tree bark. Downy woodpeckers have a built-in mask, or special feathers, near their nostrils that helps them to avoid breathing in wood chips while pecking.

Nest Type   Most Active

Hairy/Downy Woodpecker

Leuconotopicus villosus/Dryobates pubescens

Size: Hairy: 7–10 inches long; wingspan of 13–16 inches; weighs 3 ounces. Downy: 5½–7 inches long; wingspan of 10–12 inches; weighs less than an ounce

Habitat: Forested areas, parks, woodlands, and orchards

Range: Both species are year-round residents in Iowa and are found throughout the United States.

Food: Hairy: beetles, ants, caterpillars, fruits, and seeds. Downy: beetles, ants, galls, wasps, seeds, and berries

Nesting: Hairy: April to July. Downy: April to July

Nest: In both woodpecker species, pairs will work together to create a cavity. Both parents also help to incubate eggs.

Eggs: Hairy: 3–7 white eggs. Downy: 3–8 white eggs

Young: Hairy woodpeckers' eggs will hatch 2 weeks after being laid and then fledge (develop enough feathers to fly) after another month. Downy woodpeckers' eggs will hatch after about 12 days and fledge 18–21 days after hatching. Both species hatch blind and featherless.

Predators: American kestrels, snakes, sharp-shinned hawks, pet cats, rats, squirrels, and Cooper's hawks

Migration: They do not migrate.

Hairy woodpeckers and downy woodpeckers look strikingly similar with their color pattern. One way to distinguish them is to look at the size of the body and bill. The downy woodpecker is smaller than the hairy woodpecker and has a shorter bill. If you look at the tail feathers of the two species, you will also see that the hairy woodpecker does not have black spots, while the downy's tail does.

Did you know?

Cardinals are very territorial. A cardinal will sometimes attack its own reflection, thinking that another cardinal has entered its territory. The early bird gets the worm, and cardinals are some of the first birds active in the morning.

Nest Type

Most Active

Northern Cardinal
Cardinalis cardinalis

Size: 8–9 inches long; wingspan of 12 inches

Habitat: Hardwood forests, urban areas, orchards, backyards, and fields

Range: In Iowa, they are year-round residents. They are found throughout the eastern and midwestern parts of the United States.

Food: Seeds, fruits, insects, spiders, and centipedes

Nesting: March to August

Nest: The cup-shaped nest is built by females in thick foliage, usually at least 1 foot off the ground. It can be 3 inches tall and 4 inches wide.

Eggs: The female lays 2–5 off-white eggs with a variety of colored speckles.

Young: About 2 weeks after eggs are laid, chicks hatch with their eyes closed and mostly naked, aside from sparsely placed down feathers.

Predators: Hawks, owls, and squirrels

Migration: Cardinals do not migrate.

Northern cardinal males are bright-red birds with a black face. Females are a washed-out red or brown in color. Both males and females have a crest (tuft of feathers on the head), an orange beak, and grayish legs. Cardinals can be identified by their laser-gun-like call.

Did you know?

The northern harrier is the only species of harrier that lives in North America; there are 12 other species that live elsewhere. While most other hawks will hunt from a perch and then attack, northern harriers hunt on the wing, or while flying. They will sometimes even hover over prey and then pounce.

Nest Type   Most Active   Migrates

Northern Harrier

Circus cyaneus

Size: 18–19¾ inches long; wingspan of 40¼–46½ inches; weighs 10½–26½ ounces

Habitat: Open habitats such as fields, savannas, meadows, marshes, prairies, and deserts

Range: They are common in North America from Alaska down through Mexico into South America. Though common in Iowa, they are endangered and can be found during migration mostly in the northern half of the state and rarely throughout the southern half.

Food: Carnivores, they eat birds, insects, mammals, amphibians, and reptiles.

Nesting: Spring; harriers will nest alone or sometimes in colonies of 15–20 individuals.

Nest: The nest is built on the ground, many times on areas that are raised, such as clumps of dirt or grasses.

Eggs: Usually 5 bluish-white eggs are laid per clutch.

Young: Young hatch 30 days after laying. They can walk within 2 weeks and become independent within 8 weeks.

Predators: American crows, raccoons, birds of prey, red foxes, skunks, and coyotes

Migration: Migrates to breeding sites in the spring

Northern harriers have a rounded, owl-shaped face and a white patch on their rump. Adults have yellow eyes. The males have grayish backs with white undersides. The females are brown and have white stripes on their wings. Immatures have brown eyes and look like the females but are a darker shade of brown. Northern harriers have long wings and dark-tipped tails.

81

Did you know?

The osprey is nicknamed the "fish hawk" because it is the only hawk in North America that mainly eats live fish. An osprey will rotate its catch to put it in line with its body, pointing headfirst, which allows for less resistance in flight as the air travels over the fish.

Nest Type   Most Active   Migrates

Osprey
Pandion haliaetus

Size: 21–23 inches long; wingspan of 59–71 inches; weighs 3–4½ pounds

Habitat: Near lakes, ponds, rivers, swamps, and reservoirs

Range: Found in Iowa mostly as migrating residents and in some areas across the state as breeding residents; throughout Canada and the US, including Alaska

Food: Feeds mostly on fish; they sometimes eat mammals, birds, and reptiles if there are few fish.

Nesting: For ospreys that migrate, egg-laying happens in April and May. The female will take on most of the incubation of the eggs, as well as the jobs of keeping the offspring warm and providing protection.

Nest: Platform nests are constructed out of twigs and sticks. Nests are constructed on trees, snags, or human-made objects like cellular towers and telephone poles.

Eggs: The mother lays 1–3 cream-colored eggs; they have splotches of various shades of brown and pinkish red.

Young: Chicks hatch after around 36 days and have brown-and-white down feathers. Ospreys fledge around 50–55 days after hatching and will receive care from parents for another 2 months or so.

Predators: Owls, eagles, foxes, skunks, raccoons, and snakes

Migration: Ospreys migrate south to wintering areas in the fall.

Ospreys are raptors, and they have a brown upper body and white lower body. The wings are brown on the outside and white on the underside, with brown spotting and streaks toward the edge. The head is white with a brown band that goes through the eye area, highlighting the yellow eyes.

Did you know?

The red-headed woodpecker is one of few woodpecker species to not only store food, but also hide it behind bark. They rarely peck at trees for food. Instead, they will sit on a tree, fence post, or building and catch prey in the air or forage on the ground; they also pick insects from trees without digging into the bark. Red-headed woodpeckers have been known to make cavities that are over 20 inches deep in a tree.

Nest Type   Most Active

84

Red-headed Woodpecker

Melanerpes erythrocephalus

Size: 7–9 inches long; wingspan of 14–17 inches; weighs 2–3½ ounces

Habitat: Open areas such as savannas and grasslands, open woodlands, forest edges and clearings, river bottoms, and orchards

Range: They can be found in southern Canada and in the US east of the Rocky Mountains to the Atlantic Ocean, southward to Florida in the east, and to Texas in the west. In Iowa, they can be found statewide.

Food: Omnivores, they eat insects, spiders, seeds, earthworms, nuts, berries, and sometimes small mammals

Nesting: Spring

Nest: Nest in dead tree cavities that they excavate with their beaks

Eggs: 3–10 eggs, most commonly 5 eggs

Young: Chicks hatch 13 days after laying. They are naked and have eyes closed when they hatch. They are fed by both parents. They will fledge or leave the nest at around 24–31 days and are able to reproduce the following spring.

Predators: Birds of prey, snakes, foxes, flying squirrels, and racoons

Migration: Do not migrate in Iowa

The male and female red-headed woodpeckers look similar. They are made up of three colors: a red head, neck, and top of breast; deep bluish-black tails and wings; and white overall body. The lower halves of their wings also have white patches on them. Juveniles look like adults but have gray heads.

Did you know?

The red-tailed hawk is the most abundant hawk in North America. The red-tailed hawk's scream is the sound effect that you hear when soaring eagles are shown in movies. Eagles do not screech like hawks, so filmmakers use hawk calls instead! Red-tailed hawks can't move their eyes, so they have to move their entire head in order to get a better view around them.

Nest Type   Most Active

Red-tailed Hawk

Buteo jamaicensis

Size: 19–25 inches long; wingspan of 47–57 inches; weighs 2½–4 pounds

Habitat: Deserts, woodlands, grasslands, and farm fields

Range: In Iowa, they are year-round residents statewide. They are found throughout North America as year-round residents, with the exception of Canada, Alaska, portions of Mexico, northern portions of several northern and northeastern states, and Louisiana, where they are breeding or nonbreeding residents.

Food: Rodents, birds, reptiles, amphibians, bats, and insects

Nesting: Hawks mate for life; nesting starts in March.

Nest: Both the male and female help build a large cup-shaped nest, which can be over 6 feet high and 3 feet across; the nest is made of sticks and branches; nests are built at forest edges mostly in the crowns of trees, but hawks will also nest on windowsills and other human-made structures.

Eggs: 1–5 eggs; the insides of eggs are a greenish color.

Young: They start to fly after 5–6 weeks, and it takes around 10 weeks for the hatchlings to leave the nest.

Predators: Great-horned owls and crows

Migration: Populations in Iowa do not migrate.

Red-tailed hawks are named for their rusty-red tails! They have brown heads and a chest that's cream to light brown with brown streaking in the form of a band. Red-tailed hawks are highly territorial, and throughout the day they will take to the air to look for invaders.

Did you know?
Red-winged blackbirds are one of the most abundant songbirds
in the United States. Sometimes their winter roost (colony) can
have several thousand to up to a million birds. In many areas,
red-winged blackbirds are considered a pest because of their love
of grain and seeds from farm fields. In others, they are welcomed
because they eat insects that are considered pests to farmers.

Nest Type   Most Active

Red-winged Blackbird

Agelaius phoeniceus

Size: 7–9½ inches long; wingspan of 13 inches; weighs 2 ounces

Habitat: Marshes, lakeshores, meadows, parks, and open fields

Range: In Iowa, they are year-round residents. Their range extends from central Canada through the US and into Mexico.

Food: Dragonflies, spiders, beetles, snails, seeds, and fruits

Nesting: February to August

Nest: Female builds a cup from plant material.

Eggs: 3–4 eggs that come in a variety of colors, from pale blue to gray with black-and-brown spots or streaks

Young: Chicks hatch blind and naked after around 12 days of incubation. Hatchlings will leave the nest after 12 days but will continue to receive care for another 5 weeks.

Predators: Raccoons, mink, marsh wrens, owls, and raptors

Migration: They do not migrate in Iowa.

Red-winged blackbird males are a sleek black with an orangish-red spot that overlays a dandelion-yellow spot on the wings. Females have a combination of dark-brown and light-brown streaks throughout the body. Male red-winged blackbirds spend much of the breeding season defending their territory from other males and attacking predators or anything else that gets too close to the nest.

Did you know?

The sandhill crane is the most abundant crane species in the world. They are not afraid to defend themselves when threatened. They will use their feet and bill to ward off predators, often stabbing attackers with their bill. Sometimes sandhill cranes will travel 500 miles in one day to find food.

Nest Type   Most Active   Migrates

Sandhill Crane

Grus canadensis

Size: 3½–4 feet long; wingspan of 6–7 feet; weighs 7½–10 pounds

Habitat: Grasslands, savannas, and farm fields

Range: Breeding resident in western North America. They can be found during migration in many states along the multiple migration routes. Northern Iowa serves as a major resting area during migration and as breeding grounds.

Food: Berries, insects, snails, amphibians, and small mammals, as well as food crops like corn

Nesting: Nonmigratory populations will lay eggs from December–August, while populations that migrate will nest between April and May.

Nest: Both adults build the cup-shaped nest using vegetation from nearby areas.

Eggs: Up to 3 pale brownish-yellow eggs with brown spots

Young: Chicks are born with the ability to see and walk. Chicks become independent at around 9 months and will start breeding between 2 and 7 years.

Predators: Coyotes, raccoons, ravens, great horned owls, and humans

Migration: Migrate to breeding areas in the spring and south to wintering areas in the fall

The sandhill crane is a large bird with gray-to-brownish feathers with a white face and ruby-red crown. They are commonly seen in large groups in fields.

Did you know?

The trumpeter swan is the largest and heaviest waterfowl species found in North America. Trumpeter swans will use their webbed feet to aid in egg incubation. When feeding on deep aquatic plants, they will create a current in the water by pumping their feet; this current allows them to pull aquatic plants from the bottom more easily.

Nest Type	Most Active	Migrates

Trumpeter Swan

Cygnus buccinator

Size: 60–72 inches long; wingspan of 72–84 inches; weighs 17–28 pounds

Habitat: Lakes, rivers, marshes, wetlands, and coastal areas

Range: In Iowa, they can be found statewide as breeding residents. They can also be found in isolated populations throughout the northern United States and Canada.

Food: Aquatic plants, small fish, crustaceans, and fish eggs

Nesting: March to May

Nest: Both male and female swans construct the circular nest. Nest-building can take 2–5 weeks to complete.

Eggs: 4–6 cream or white eggs

Young: Young hatch 32–37 days after eggs are laid; they leave the nest after a day and can fly after around 100 days. They are independent at around 10 months and reach full maturity between 4 and 7 years.

Predators: Eagles, owls, coyotes, mink, otters, and ravens

Migration: They migrate south during the fall to wintering grounds, and north in the spring to breeding grounds.

Adult trumpeter swans are large white birds with long necks, black bills, and webbed feet; juveniles (young) are a grayish color. Trumpeter swans are only found in North America. They have a thick layer of down feathers that aid in living in cold areas.

Did you know?

Turkey vultures help prevent the spread of diseases by feeding on dead animals before they rot. They are not able to kill their own prey due to how their feet are structured. Turkey vultures have something most birds don't: a good sense of smell; in fact, they have the largest smelling (or olfactory) system of any bird. They can smell food from up to a mile away.

Nest Type   Most Active   Migrates

Turkey Vulture

Cathartes aura

Size: 25¼–32 inches long; wingspan is 66–70 inches; weighs 4⅜ pounds

Habitat: Forests, woodland edges, cities, farmland

Range: Turkey vultures can be found throughout the southern United States as well as in the northern US during the breeding season. In Iowa, they are found statewide as breeding residents.

Food: Carrion (dead animals) like deer, snakes, and coyotes.

Nesting: Secluded caves, cliff ledges, hollow trees, abandoned nests of other large birds. They nest in secluded areas that are distant from humans.

Nest: A simple "scrape" nest of discarded plants or wood

Eggs: 1–3 creamy-white, speckled eggs

Young: Chicks are born 28–40 days or so after laying. They are born blind with down feathers. Chicks fledge 70 days after hatching and are independent a week or so afterward.

Predators: Raccoons, opossums, and foxes prey on eggs. Snakes, eagles, hawks, and owls may attack juveniles or sick or injured adults. Healthy adults are rarely prey.

Migration: Those in the northern US migrate south.

Turkey vultures look all black, but up close, they are different shades of light gray and brown. Turkey vultures have a red head. Turkey vultures make a black "T" shape when in flight and have light-gray undersides on their wings/tail.

Did you know?

Turkeys sometimes fly at night, unlike most birds, and land in trees to roost. Turkeys have some interesting facial features; the red skin growth on a turkey's face above the beak is called a snood, while the growth under the beak is called a wattle. Wild turkeys can have more than 5,000 feathers.

Nest Type   Most Active

Wild Turkey

Meleagris gallopavo

Size: 3–4 feet long; wingspan of 5 feet; males weigh 16–25 pounds; females weigh 9–11 pounds.

Habitat: Woodlands and grasslands

Range: In Iowa, they are year-round residents. They also can be found in the eastern US and have been introduced in many western areas of the country.

Food: Grain, snakes, frogs, insects, acorns, berries, and ferns

Nesting: April to September

Nest: The nest is built on the ground using leaves as bedding, in brush or near the base of trees or fallen logs.

Eggs: 10–12 tan eggs with very small reddish-brown spots

Young: Poults (young) hatch about a month after eggs are laid; they will flock with the mother for a year. When young are still unable to fly, the mom will stay on the ground with her poults to provide protection and warmth. When poults grow up, they are known as hens if they are female, or as gobblers or toms if they are male.

Predators: Humans, foxes, raccoons, owls, eagles, skunks, and fishers

Migration: Turkeys do not migrate.

A wild turkey is a large bird that is dark brown and black with some iridescent feathers. Males will fan out their tail to attract a mate. When threatened, they will also fan out their tail and rush the predator, sometimes kicking and puncturing prey with the spurs on their feet.

Did you know?

Wood ducks will "mimic" a soccer player when a predator is near their young: they flop! Female wood ducks will fake a broken wing to lure predators away from her young. Wood duck hatchlings must jump from the nest after hatching to reach the water. They can jump 50 feet or more without hurting themselves.

Nest Type

Most Active

Migrates

Wood Duck

Aix sponsa

Size: 15–20 inches long; wingspan of 30 inches; weighs about a pound

Habitat: Swamps, woody ponds, and marshes

Range: They are year-long residents throughout Iowa. They are also in the eastern US, southern Mexico, the Pacific Northwest, and on the West Coast.

Food: Fruits; nuts; and aquatic vegetation, especially duckweed, sedges, and grasses

Nesting: March to August

Nest: Wood ducks use hollow trees, abandoned woodpecker cavities, and human-made nesting boxes.

Eggs: 8–15 off-white eggs are laid once a year. Sometimes females will lay eggs in another female's nest; this process is called egg dumping.

Young: Eggs hatch about a month after being laid. Chicks will leave the nest after a day and fly within 8 weeks.

Predators: Raccoons, mink, fish, hawks, snapping turtles, owls, humans, and muskrats

Migration: They do not migrate.

Wood duck males have a brightly colored crest (tuft of feathers) of iridescent (shimmering) green, red, and purple, with a mahogany (brown) upper breast area and tan bottom. Males also have red eyes. Females are brown to gray. Wood ducks have strong claws that enable them to climb up trees into cavities.

Did you know?

Yellow-billed cuckoos are one of the few bird species that can eat hairy caterpillars. They will sometimes lay their eggs in the nests of other cuckoos—and even other bird species. They do not lay all their eggs at once; instead, they lay one at a time, allowing the chick from the oldest egg to hatch and leave the nest before the last egg hatches.

Nest Type

Most Active

Migrates

Yellow-billed Cuckoo

Coccyzus americanus

Size: 10¼–11¾ inches long; wingspan of 15–17 inches; weighs 2–2¼ ounces

Habitat: Forests, meadows, woodlands, scrubby areas, thickets along streams, marshes, overgrown orchards, and abandoned farmland

Range: They can be found throughout most of the US, with higher concentrations from South Dakota to Texas and eastward to the Atlantic Coast. There are also isolated populations of the birds farther out west. They can be found statewide in Iowa as breeding residents.

Food: Beetles, ants, fruits, seeds, spiders, frogs, lizards, and caterpillars

Nesting: April to September

Nest: The male and female build a platform nest that is around 5 inches across and 1½ inches deep.

Eggs: 1–5 bluish-green or greenish-yellow eggs are laid per brood.

Young: Chicks hatch 9–11 days after laying, with just a few feathers and eyes closed. They can fledge within 8 days.

Predators: Birds of prey, snakes, chipmunks, and smaller birds

Migration: Migrate from wintering grounds in South and Central America to the US during spring

Yellow-billed cuckoos are slender birds with long tails. They are brown on their backs and sides with a white underside. They have a black face mask with yellow eye-rings and a large, curved bill. Their outer wings are red to rusty brown. They have white spots on the underside of their tail.

Did you know?

Yellow-rumped warblers are sometimes referred to as "butter butts" because of the yellow patch just above their tail feathers. The yellow-rumped warbler is the only warbler that is able to eat and digest waxy berries from wax myrtle trees. Yellow-rumped warblers are often the first warblers to return in the spring to their breeding grounds.

Nest Type

Most Active

Migrates

Yellow-rumped Warbler

Setophaga coronata

Size: 4¾–5½ inches long; wingspan of 7½–9 inches; weighs ⅖–½ ounces

Habitat: Mountainous areas, forests, open woods, parks, shrubby areas, coastal areas, and farm fields

Range: They are found across North America throughout the year and statewide in Iowa as breeding residents.

Food: Insects such as aphids, ants, beetles, and grasshoppers, as well as spiders and berries from plants like poison ivy, dogwood, and wax myrtles

Nesting: Late March to May

Nest: Females build a cup-shaped nest out of grass, twigs, roots, and even fur. The cup is lined with fur and feathers. The nest is 2 inches tall and 3–4 inches across.

Eggs: 1–6 white or reddish-brown eggs with brown specks

Young: Chicks hatch almost naked with spots of down and are totally reliant on parents about 13 days after laying. They will fledge from the nest in about 14 days.

Predators: Snakes, crows, cats, foxes, raccoons, raptors, and weasels

Migration: Migrates north to the breeding areas in the spring, and south to the overwintering grounds in the fall

Breeding males are blue gray with black streaks. Their shoulders, rump, and a strip of the top of their head are bright yellow. They have white undersides and wing bars, plus black streaking on their chest and sides. Breeding females look similar to males but are not as bright and have less black side streaking. Nonbreeding birds are pale brown in color with a yellow rump and sides.

Did you know?

The American toad is the most commonly observed toad in Iowa. While the American toad has warts on it, you cannot get warts from touching it. Toads are toxic (but not to humans); they have two parotid glands—one behind each eye that produces a toxin they release to prevent predators from eating them.

Most Active   Hibernates

American Toad

Anaxyrus americanus

Size: 2–4 inches long; weighs 1½–2 ounces

Habitat: Prairies, forests, suburban areas, swamps, and other wetlands

Range: They are found statewide in Iowa and New England, and south into parts of Mississippi, Alabama, and Georgia.

Food: Insects, worms, snails, ants, moths, and beetles

Mating: February to July

Nest: No nest

Eggs: 2,000–19,000 or more eggs are laid in bodies of water attached to vegetation or the bottom of shallow water.

Young: Eggs hatch 3–10 days after laying. They will stay in the tadpole stage 40–65 days. It takes 2–3 years to reach reproductive maturity.

Predators: Hognoses and other snakes, raccoons, and birds; as tadpoles: beetles, crayfish, birds, and dragonfly larvae

The American toad has a brown-to-clay-red-colored base layer with brown and black spots and noticeable warts on its body. During the summer or extreme heat, toads can reduce their metabolic rate and cool themselves down.

Did you know?
Blue-spotted salamanders spend most of the year under leaves and even in underground burrows. They migrate long distances to their breeding areas. The population in Iowa is actually isolated (or cut off from) the rest of the population in the eastern United States.

Most Active

Hibernates

Blue-spotted Salamander

Ambystoma laterale

Size: 4–5½ inches long; weighs under an ounce

Habitat: Swamps, marshes, burrows under logs, and temporary pools in forests

Range: They can be found in Canada down into New England and westward through Ohio, Michigan, Minnesota, and a few other states. In Iowa, they can only be found in Linn and Black Hawk Counties.

Food: They are carnivores that eat invertebrates like snails, spiders, worms, insects, and slugs.

Mating: Early spring

Nest: No nest is made, but eggs are deposited on the bottom of temporary pools (also called vernal ponds or pools) usually under leaves, rocks, or other types of debris.

Eggs: Up to 500 eggs are laid one by one or in scattered clusters underneath submerged leaves.

Young: Larvae hatch within a month and live in the pond until they go through metamorphosis (change into a salamander) later in the year.

Predators: Snakes, birds, frogs, turtles, raccoons, and skunks

Blue-spotted salamanders have black bodies with grayish-blue spots on their back, tail, and sides of their body.

Did you know?

The mudpuppy is Iowa's only fully aquatic salamander, meaning that it never leaves the water. Mudpuppies are neotenic, meaning they are the result of incomplete metamorphosis where they remain in their larval state. They are one of the few species of salamanders that make a noise. It was once believed that they could bark, which is where the name mudpuppy comes from; however, the sound is more of a grunt or squeak than a true bark.

Most Active

Common Mudpuppy

Necterus maculosus

Size: 8–17 inches long; weighs up to 8 ounces

Habitat: Aquatic habitats such as ponds, lakes, streams, creeks, and rivers with plenty of shelter or places to hide

Range: They are found from Canada southward to Georgia and Louisiana, and as far west as North Dakota. In Iowa, they can be found in the eastern portion of the state.

Food: They are carnivores that eat fish, crayfish, insects, spiders, worms, and mussels.

Mating: Fall; they will not lay eggs until the following spring.

Nest: Nests are dug under rocks or logs submerged in water. Eggs are attached to the roof of the nest or underside of the log or object that the nest is dug under.

Eggs: Around 100 eggs are laid in spring, often one by one.

Young: Larvae hatch around 1–2 months later. They have gills and a smaller tail. They will reach reproductive maturity at 4–6 years old.

Predators: Snakes, wading birds like egrets and herons, and fish

Mudpuppies are salamanders that live their entire lives in water, never touching land. They are brown to grayish with dark spots on their back and a lighter-gray underside. They have a big, flattened head; small, square snout; and large external gills that are deep red to bright ruby in color. Gills are bushy and extend from the side of the neck before the first set of legs. Gills are larger depending on where they live (usually those in slow-to-nonmoving waters will have larger gills than the ones in faster currents). Juveniles are smaller and darker in color with a pale-yellow-to-off-white stripe flowing down the body.

Did you know?

The snapping turtle's sex is determined by the temperature of the nest! Nest temperatures that are 67–68 degrees produce females, temperatures in the range between 70 and 72 degrees produce both males and females, and nests that are 73–75 degrees will usually produce all males.

Most Active

Common Snapping Turtle

Chelydra serpentina

Size: 8–16 inches long; weighs 10–35 pounds

Habitat: Rivers, marshes, and lakes; can be found in areas that have brackish water (freshwater and saltwater mixture)

Range: They are found statewide in Iowa; they're also found in the eastern US and southern Canada.

Food: These omnivores (eaters of both plants and animals) eat frogs, reptiles, snakes, birds, small mammals, and plants.

Mating: April to November are the breeding months; lays eggs during June and July.

Nest: Females dig a hole in sandy soil and lay the eggs into it.

Eggs: 25–42 eggs, sometimes as many as 80 or more

Young: Like sea turtles, snapping turtles have temperature-dependent sex determination (TSD), meaning the temperature of the nest determines the sex of the young. Hatchlings leave the nest between August and October. In the North, turtles mature at around 15–20 years, while southern turtles mature around 12 years old.

Predators: Raccoons, skunks, crows, dogs, and humans

The snapping turtle's carapace (top shell) is dark green to brown and usually covered in algae or moss. The plastron (bottom shell) is smaller than the carapace. They are crepuscular animals that are mostly active during the dawn and dusk hours. Young turtles will actively look for food. As adults, they rely heavily on ambushing to hunt; they bury themselves in the sand with just the tip of their nose and eyes showing.

Did you know?

Copperheads get their name from their copper- to bronze-colored head. A copperhead's size can give a hint to how large its fangs are. The larger or longer the snake, the longer the fangs usually are. Young copperheads are born with a bright-yellow tail that aids the young snake in catching prey. The snake moves its tail around like a worm to lure would-be prey.

Most Active   Hibernates

Safety Note: This snake is venomous (toxic). If you see one, observe or admire it from a distance.

Copperhead
Agkistrodon contortrix

Size: 22–40 inches long; weighs 4–10 ounces or larger

Habitat: Dry rocky hillsides, lowland forest areas, grasslands, water-adjacent wooded areas, and suburban areas

Range: They live throughout the eastern and central US. They can be found in the southeastern corner of Iowa, but they are extremely rare.

Food: Mice, rats, baby cottontails, small birds, swamp rabbits, lizards, baby turtles, small snakes, amphibians, and insects

Mating: April to May and late August to October. Males produce a pheromone that makes the female unattractive to other males.

Nest: Copperheads do not make nests but utilize natural dens or dens made by other animals. Dens are often near water sources, in rock crevices, hollowed-out logs or downed trees, or in shrub piles.

Eggs: Copperheads are ovoviviparous: the eggs develop in the body, and the mother then gives live birth.

Young: Females give live birth to 5–8 (sometimes 20) 6–10-inch-long young. These snakes reach reproductive maturity at 4 years. They are independent at birth.

Predators: Snakes, raptors, raccoons, and opossums

Copperheads have a triangular or arrow-like, copper-bronze head. Eyes have vertical tear-shaped pupils. The thick body comes in varieties of tans, browns, dirty oranges, and copper. They have 10–18 hourglass-shaped bands. Copperheads are the only species with this hourglass shape. Juveniles have the same pattern but fewer hourglass shapes. They also have a yellow-tipped tail that fades away by age 3 or 4.

Did you know?

Eastern garter snakes are highly social and will form groups with other snakes and often other species to overwinter together in a burrow or hole. When threatened by a predator or handled, they will sometimes musk or emit a foul-smelling, oily substance from their cloaca (butt).

Most Active   Hibernates

Eastern Garter Snake

Thamnophis sirtalis

Size: 14–36 inches long (rarely over 17 inches); weighs 5–5½ ounces

Habitat: Forests and forest edges, grasslands, and suburban areas

Range: They are found statewide in Iowa and can be found in the eastern US from Minnesota, southward to eastern Texas, and then east towards the Atlantic coast.

Food: Frogs, snails, toads, salamanders, insects, fish, and worms

Mating: April or May

Nest: No nest; they will use natural cavities in the ground or abandoned burrows of small mammals.

Eggs: No eggs are laid. Eastern garter snakes are born live in a litter of 8–20 snakes.

Young: Snakelets are 4½–9 inches long at birth; no parental care is given.

Predators: Crows, ravens, hawks, owls, raccoons, foxes, and squirrels

Eastern garter snakes are black with three yellow stripes running down their body on the back and sides. They withstand winter by gathering in groups inside the burrows of rodents or under human-made structures, and they enter brumation, or a state of slowed body activity.

Did you know?

The eastern hognose snake is venomous! But its venom is not harmful to us. The hognose's teeth have a dual purpose: they inject venom into prey and also deflate toads who puff their bodies up to avoid being eaten. The hognose wards off would-be predators by flattening its head to look like a cobra. If that doesn't work, it will play dead by flipping its body over and letting its tongue hang out of its mouth.

Most Active   Hibernates

Eastern Hognose Snake

Heterodon platirhinos

Size: 2–2½ feet long; weighs 2–4 ounces

Habitat: Shrublands, prairies, grasslands, coastal areas, and forests

Range: The hognose can be found in the southern parts of Iowa. It has an expansive range southward into Florida and westward into Texas and parts of Kansas.

Food: Frogs, toads, salamanders, birds, and invertebrates

Mating: April and May

Nest: Eastern hognose snakes dig burrows and will lay eggs under rocks, leaves, or in rotting logs.

Eggs: In June to July they will dig a burrow and lay 8–40 eggs (average clutch is around 25).

Young: 60 days after being laid, the eggs hatch. They do not receive care from parents at birth. Snakes reach full maturity around 20 months.

Predators: Hawks, snakes, raccoons, and opossums

The eastern hognose is a thick-bodied snake that gets its name from its shovel-like snout that it uses to dig in soil. They come in a variety of colors from red and brown to gray and black; they even come in versions of orange and red. Their underbody is lighter than their top.

Did you know?

They are called milk snakes because they are often found in barns with cows. It was once believed that they were drinking the milk of the cows; in reality, they were feeding on the mice and other rodents in the barn. Milk snakes have one of the largest ranges of all snakes; they can be found from Canada into Mexico and even Central America.

Most Active   Hibernates

Eastern Milk Snake

Lampropeltis triangulum

Size: 19–40 inches long; weighs 1½–8 ounces

Habitat: Suburban parks, fields, woodlands, swamps, bogs, marshes, rocky outcrops, pastures, and farm areas

Range: In Iowa, they are found statewide. They are found from southeastern Canada down to Florida and as far west as Arizona and Utah.

Food: Birds and bird eggs, slugs, small mammals, and other snakes

Mating: Spring, during June or July

Nest: No nest is made; eggs are laid in loose soil or logs.

Eggs: 4–12 off-white-to-creamy, oval-shaped eggs are laid.

Young: After 1½–2 months, young will hatch.

Predators: Birds of prey, snakes, coyotes, foxes, and skunks; humans will kill them due to misidentifying them as venomous snakes.

Eastern milk snakes are small, slender-bodied snakes. They have a narrow head with a Y- or V-shaped patch at the base where their neck starts. Adults will have between three and five rows of reddish or brown blotching down their back. They have a black-and-white checkerboard pattern on their belly. Young are brightly colored with red blotches, but they lose that brightness as they get older.

Did you know?

The eastern tiger salamander can grow up to 13 inches long and live over 20 years! Eastern tiger salamanders migrate to their birthplace in order to breed, sometimes over a mile or more. Eastern tiger salamanders have a hidden weapon! They produce a poisonous toxin that is secreted or released from two glands in their tail. This toxin makes them taste bad to predators and allows them to escape.

Most Active   Hibernates

Eastern Tiger Salamander

Ambystoma tigrinum

Size: 7–13 inches long; weighs 4½ ounces

Habitat: Woodlands, marshes, and meadows; they spend most of their time underground in burrows.

Range: Mostly found in the eastern US. In Iowa, they can be found statewide, with more sightings in the eastern parts of the state. Small populations are also found in the western US.

Food: Carnivores (eaters of meat), they eat insects, frogs, worms, and snails.

Mating: Tiger salamanders leave their burrows to find standing bodies of freshwater. They breed in late winter and early spring after the ground has thawed.

Nest: No nest, but eggs are joined together into one group in a jelly-like sack called an egg mass. An egg mass is attached to grass, leaves, and other plant material at the bottom of a pond.

Eggs: There are 20–100 eggs or more in an egg mass.

Young: Eggs hatch after 2 weeks, and the young are fully aquatic with external gills. Limbs develop shortly after hatching; within 3 months, the young are fully grown but will hang around in a vernal pool. Individuals living in permanent ponds can take up to 6 months to fully develop.

Predators: Adults: snakes, owls, and badgers; young: diving beetles, fish, turtles, and herons

Eastern tiger salamanders have thick black, brown, or grayish bodies with uneven spots of yellow, tan, brown, or green along the head and body. The underside is usually a variation of yellow. Males are usually larger and thicker than females.

Did you know?

Five-lined skinks get their name from the five stripes or lines that run down their body. It's a myth that young five-lines are poisonous; while they are not poisonous, their blue color could be used to trick predators into believing that they taste bad. Another use for the blue tail is to act as a distraction. When the five-lined skink is caught, it can drop its tail, and the flopping, brightly colored tail can help aid in its escape.

Most Active   Hibernates

Five-lined Skink

Plestiodon fasciatus

Size: 5–8½ inches long; weighs 4½ ounces

Habitat: Forests, rocky areas, woodlands, and wetlands

Range: They can be found along the counties of the eastern part of the state in Iowa and throughout the eastern United States to Florida, west to Texas, and as far north as Canada.

Food: Carnivores (eaters of meat), they eat spiders, newborn mice, frogs, beetles and other insects, and lizards.

Mating: May to July

Nest: Cavity nests are usually made in rotten logs, stumps, rocks, and bark.

Eggs: Lays 15–18 eggs

Young: 4–6 weeks after incubation, the 2–2½-inch-long young hatch. Young are independent at hatching but will receive care and protection for 1–2 days until they leave the nest. Skinks become mature 2–3 years after hatching.

Predators: Birds such as crows, American kestrels, shrikes, and hawks; cats, foxes, raccoons, shrews, snakes, and moles

When young, five-lined skinks are dark brown to black with five yellow-to-off-white lines on their back that run to the base of the tail. Their tail is a brilliant blue. The color of the tail fades as they age, and the lines change from yellow to brown (and some are almost completely gone). The dark-brown color fades, too, and older individuals are often brownish with faint lines. During breeding season, males will don a reddish-orange chin.

Did you know?
Leopard frogs are used by humans in many ways, including in research for medical projects and as specimens for biology courses. During the winter, they will hibernate underwater in ponds that have lots of oxygen and do not freeze.

Most Active   Hibernates

Northern Leopard Frog

Lithobates pipiens

Size: 2½–4½ inches long; weighs ½–3 ounces

Habitat: Meadows, open fields, lakes, forest edges, and ponds

Range: In Iowa, they are found statewide; there are strong populations into Canada and throughout the north-eastern states, with populations extending into northern California, the Pacific Northwest, and the Southwest.

Food: Spiders, worms, insects, and other invertebrates like crustaceans and mollusks

Mating: Late March to early June; mating occurs in water.

Nest: No nest is constructed; within 3 days of mating, the female will lay eggs in permanent shallow bodies of water, attached to vegetation just below the surface.

Eggs: A few hundred to 7,000 or more eggs are laid in one egg mass that is 2–5 inches wide.

Young: Tadpoles hatch about 2–3 weeks after eggs are laid and then complete the metamorphic cycle to become frogs in around 3 months. They reach reproductive maturity in the first or second year for males and within 2–3 years for females.

Predators: Fish, frogs, herons, snakes, hawks, gulls, mink, turtles, and dragonfly larvae

The northern leopard frog is a smooth-skinned frog with 2–3 rows of dark spots with a lighter outline around them, atop a brown or green base layer. It has a ridge that extends from the base of the eye to the rear of the frog. They have a white underside. Juveniles (young) will use streams and drainage ditches with vegetation to reach seasonal habitats.

Did you know?

Northern map turtles get their name from the map-like pattern on their carapace. They are the most abundant map turtle species in the United States. They are social animals and can be found basking in the sun with other turtles. During the winter, they will hibernate in deeper bodies of water.

Most Active   Hibernates

Northern Map Turtle

Graptemys geographica

Size: Female: 7–10¾ inches long; male: 3½–6¼ inches long; weighs 5 ounces–1 pound

Habitat: Ponds, lakes, wetlands, rivers, and reservoirs that have good basking areas

Range: In Iowa, they are found in the eastern portion of the state. They can be found as far north as Canada, southward to Alabama, and westward to Oklahoma.

Food: Snails, aquatic insects, crayfish, mussels, and fish

Mating: Spring and fall

Nest: Nests are built on sandy and loose soil, beaches, or sand bars that are close to the water.

Eggs: Clutch size is usually 10–12 eggs

Young: Around 75 days after laying, young will hatch. The sex of the young is determined by temperature; hotter nests produce more females and cooler nests produce more males. They are independent at hatching and receive no parental care. They reach reproductive maturity at around 4 years for males and 10 or more years for females.

Predators: Racoons, river otters, crows, skunks, foxes, and coyotes

The northern map turtle has a carapace (top shell) that is black or dark greenish in color. Young turtles have a pattern that resembles the lines on a map. The pattern fades as they get older. Both males and females have a paler plastron (bottom shell) and webbed feet. They have a dark-colored head that has yellow-to-white lines down their face and a small yellow spot just below each eye. Males are smaller than females and possess a ridge or keel down their back. Females' keels are not as noticeable, and they have a larger head with a strong jaw.

Did you know?

The spadefoot toad is actually a frog! Its smooth skin is one thing that gives it away! Spadefoot toads get their name from the spade-like appendages on their hind feet that they use to dig burrows. Spadefoots can produce a toxin through their skin to ward off would-be predators. Spadefoots are the only amphibians in Iowa with vertical pupils.

Most Active   Hibernates

Plains Spadefoot Toad

Spea bombifrons

Size: 1½–2 inches long; weighs 1 ounce

Habitat: Grasslands, flooded fields, ponds, areas with loose soil, farm fields, savannas, sandhills, and scrublands

Range: In Iowa, they are found along the counties of the western border. They can be found from southern Canada down into Montana and the central portion of the US, including the Dakotas, as well as southward to Texas, Oklahoma, and Arizona.

Food: They are carnivores that eat insects and worms.

Mating: April through August after heavy rains

Nest: No nest; eggs are laid in water attached to submerged plants.

Eggs: Eggs are laid in clusters from a dozen to over 200. Eggs are dark brown and surrounded by layers of jelly.

Young: Larvae or tadpoles hatch about 2 days after laying. They will go through metamorphosis and turn into frogs in about 14–20 days. They reach reproductive maturity in 2 years.

Predators: Owls, snakes, rodents, crayfish, and, as larvae, beetles

Plains spadefoot toads are small amphibians. They have big eyes and short hind legs. Each foot of the hind legs has a wedge-like or spade-shaped appendage on it. Their skin is grayish to tan and brown with a palish-to-white underside. They have brown-to-black markings on their back, with warts or bumps of red. Sometimes, they also have pale-brown stripes down their back.

Did you know?

Spiny softshell turtles will bury themselves under a layer of mud at the bottom of a lake, with only their head sticking out, and catch prey as it passes by. In addition to breathing through their lungs, they can extract oxygen from the water through their skin; this aids them in being able to stay underwater for over 4 hours.

Most Active

Spiny Softshell Turtle

Apalone spinifera

Size: Females: 7–19 inches long (carapace); males: 5–10 inches long; females weigh 20–30 pounds, while males are considerably smaller.

Habitat: Sand bars, lakes, rivers, wetlands, and city areas

Range: In North America, they can be found as far north as Canada and as far south as Mexico. They can be found in South Carolina and Georgia and as far west as California. In Iowa, they can be found almost statewide.

Food: Aquatic insects, fish, snails, tadpoles, and crayfish

Mating: Mating takes place in the spring.

Nest: Eggs are buried in a flask-shaped chamber that is around 4–10 inches deep, along rivers, in sand bars, or on loose soils on banks.

Eggs: 4–38 white eggs are laid per clutch.

Young: Young hatch between 65–85 days after laying. Young turtles are about 1½ inches long at hatching. While in other turtle species the sex of hatchlings is determined by temperature, in spiny softshell turtles, it is determined by genetics. Females become reproductively mature at around ages 8–9, while males become mature at around age 4.

Predators: Raccoons, herons, large fish, and foxes

Spiny softshell turtles are brown-to-olive, flat-shaped turtles with dark spots on their back and limbs. They have a long, snorkel-like nose and webbed feet. The front of the carapace has spines and bumps. Females are larger than males, but males have longer and thicker tails. Their shell is leathery and lacks scutes or scales. The underside, or plastron, is cream or yellow.

Did you know?

Spring peepers get their name because their chirp call usually coordinates with the beginning of spring. They are able to prevent their blood from freezing during the winter due to an adaptation in their blood that acts like antifreeze. Spring peepers' calls or chirps can be heard over a mile away!

Most Active   Hibernates

Spring Peeper

Pseudacris crucifer

Size: About 1–1½ inches long; weighs about as much as a penny

Habitat: Woodlands, forest edges, suburban areas, ponds, swamps, and other wetlands

Range: Widespread throughout the state of Massachusetts; their range extends throughout northeastern Canada downward to north Florida and eastward into east Texas.

Food: Insects

Mating: Their mating takes place between March and June, in or near ponds and other bodies of still water.

Nest: No nest building occurs. Eggs are laid and then attached to underwater vegetation and debris at the bottom of shallow ponds.

Eggs: They typically lay 800–1,000 eggs; each egg is covered in a jelly-like coat.

Young: 3–4 days after egg laying, eggs will hatch into tadpoles. Over the next 7–8 weeks, tadpoles will go through a transformation called metamorphosis and turn into frogs.

Predators: Birds (especially herons and raptors), fish, snakes, rats, and otters

The spring peeper is usually some shade of brown or tan. It has darker line-like markings on its back. Spring peepers are more active during the night, when the darkness provides extra protection from the fewer predators that are out at that time.

Did you know?

When threatened, a timber rattlesnake will shake its rattle to warn would-be predators. These snakes are venomous (their bites inject toxin, **so do not go near one or try to pick one up!** Instead, leave it alone so it can help people by munching on rodents and other pests. Rattlesnakes are "pit vipers," snakes that have a special body part located between the eye and mouth that helps them "see" heat.

Most Active   Hibernates

Timber Rattlesnake

Crotalus horridus

Size: 36–40 inches long; weighs 1–2 pounds

Habitat: Lowland forests and hilly wooded areas near water

Range: Their range extends as far north as New Hampshire and as far west as central Texas. In Iowa, they can be found in the eastern part of the state.

Food: Rabbits, squirrels, rats, mice, birds, other snakes, lizards, and frogs

Mating: September to January; mating occurs in the summer and fall. Males compete for females and display a courtship "dance."

Nest: The mother gives birth in a burrow or hollow log.

Eggs: They are ovoviviparous, so snakes are born live.

Young: Females give birth to 12 or more young that are around 10–18 inches long.

Predators: Coyotes, bobcats, skunks, foxes, hawks, and owls; kingsnakes, indigo snakes, and cottonmouths

Adult timber rattlesnakes are gray with a brown-to-pink hue. They have brown or orange stripes that run down their back. Their tail is usually black. A distinguishing feature is the bold black chevron symbol (like a widened V) that runs down their back, with the head of the V facing toward their head. They have catlike pupils that are vertical or elliptical in shape. Young look like the adults but are lighter and have a shorter rattle.

Did you know?

The western glass lizard look like a snake because it lacks legs. A few characteristics that let us know it is a lizard are that it has eyelids that move (snakes do not have eyelids) and it has equal or more tail than its total body length. Western glass lizards get their name from how their tails detach when they are scared or captured. The detached tail separates from the body, making it look like the lizard has shattered into pieces.

Most Active

Western Slender Glass Lizard

Ophisaurus attenuatus attenuatus

Size: 20–40 inches long; weighs 11–21 ounces

Habitat: Prairies, oak savannas, rocky hillsides, forests, and open grassy areas

Range: In Iowa, they are found in the southeastern corner of the state that borders Indiana. They are found from western Kansas to central Indiana and south through Missouri to southern Texas.

Food: They are carnivores that eat small mice, grasshoppers, spiders, beetles, and the eggs of reptiles and birds.

Mating: Takes place in spring

Nest: Nests are usually depressions in sandy soil or under natural covering. The female will guard the eggs until they hatch.

Eggs: 5–15 eggs are laid in June and July.

Young: In August, the 7-inch, khaki-to-beige-colored young with dark stripes along each side hatch. The young are independent at hatching.

Predators: Hawks, raccoons, foxes, coyotes, bobcats, skunks, and several snake species

Slender glass lizards are legless lizards. They are tan or brown, often with black stripes down their back and sides, with a cream-colored underside. They have eyelids and external ear openings.

Glossary

Adaptation—An animal's physical (outward) or behavioral (inward) adjustment to changes in the environment.

Amphibian—A small animal with a backbone, has moist skin, and lacks scales. Most amphibians start out as an egg, live at least part of their life in water, and finish life as a land dweller.

Biome—A part or region of Earth that has a particular type of climate and animals and plants that adapted to live in the area.

Bird—A group of animals that all have two legs and feet, a beak, feathers, and wings; while not all birds fly, all birds lay eggs.

Brood—A group of young birds that hatch at the same time and with the same mother.

Carnivore—An animal that primarily eats other animals.

Clutch—The number of eggs an animal lays during one nesting period; an animal can lay more than one clutch each season.

Crepuscular—The hours before sunset or just after sunrise; some animals have adapted to be most active during these low-light times.

Diurnal—During the day; many animals are most active during the daytime.

Ecosystem—A group of animals and plants that interact with each other and the physical area that they live in.

Evolution—A process of change in a species or a group of animals that are all the same kind; evolution happens over several generations or in a group of animals living around the same time; evolution happens through adaptation, or physical and biological changes to better fit the environment over time.

Fledgling—A baby bird that has developed flight feathers and has left the nest.

Gestation—The length of time a developing animal is carried in its mother's womb.

Herbivore—An animal that primarily eats plants.

Hibernate—A survival strategy or process where animals "slow down" and go into a long period of reduced activity to survive winter or seasonal changes; during hibernation, activities like feeding, breathing, and converting food to energy all stop.

Insectivore—An animal whose diet consists of insects.

Incubate—When a bird warms eggs by sitting on them.

Invasive—A nonnative animal that outcompetes native animals in a particular area, harming the environment.

Mammal—An air-breathing, warm-blooded, fur- or hair-covered animal with a backbone. All mammals produce milk and usually give birth to live young.

Migration—When animals move from one area to another. Migration usually occurs seasonally, but it can also happen due to biological processes, such as breeding.

Molt—When animals shed or drop their skin, feathers, or shell.

Nocturnal—At night; many animals are most active at night.

Piscivore—An animal that eats mainly fish.

Predator—An animal that hunts (and eats) other animals.

Raptor—A group of birds that all have a curved beak and sharp talons; they hunt or feed on other animals. Also known as a bird of prey.

Reptile—An egg-laying, air-breathing, cold-blooded animal that has a backbone and skin made of scales, which crawls on its belly or uses stubby legs to get around.

Scat—The waste product that animals release from their bodies; another word for it is poop or droppings.

Talon—The claw on the feet seen on raptors and birds of prey.

Torpor—A form of hibernation in which an animal slows down its breathing and heart rate; torpor ranges from a few hours at a time to a whole day; torpor does not involve a deep sleep.

Checklist

Mammals

- [ ] American Badger
- [ ] American Beaver
- [ ] American Mink
- [ ] Big Brown Bat
- [ ] Bobcat
- [ ] Coyote
- [ ] Eastern Chipmunk
- [ ] Eastern Cottontail
- [ ] Eastern Fox Squirrel
- [ ] Long-tailed Weasel
- [ ] Muskrat
- [ ] Northern Raccoon
- [ ] Northern River Otter
- [ ] Red Fox
- [ ] Southern Flying Squirrel
- [ ] Striped Skunk
- [ ] Thirteen-lined Ground Squirrel
- [ ] Tricolored Bat
- [ ] Virginia Opossum
- [ ] White-tailed Deer
- [ ] White-tailed Jackrabbit
- [ ] Woodchuck (Groundhog)

Birds

- [ ] American Goldfinch
- [ ] American Robin
- [ ] Bald Eagle
- [ ] Barred Owl
- [ ] Belted Kingfisher
- [ ] Black-capped Chickadee
- [ ] Blue Jay
- [ ] Blue-winged Teal
- [ ] Great Blue Heron
- [ ] Great Horned Owl
- [ ] Hairy/Downy Woodpecker
- [ ] Northern Cardinal
- [ ] Northern Harrier
- [ ] Osprey
- [ ] Red-headed Woodpecker
- [ ] Red-tailed Hawk
- [ ] Red-winged Blackbird
- [ ] Sandhill Crane
- [ ] Trumpeter Swan
- [ ] Turkey Vulture
- [ ] Wild Turkey
- [ ] Wood Duck
- [ ] Yellow-billed Cuckoo
- [ ] Yellow-rumped Warbler

Reptiles and Amphibians

- ☐ American Toad
- ☐ Blue-spotted Salamander
- ☐ Common Mudpuppy
- ☐ Common Snapping Turtle
- ☐ Copperhead
- ☐ Eastern Garter Snake
- ☐ Eastern Hognose Snake
- ☐ Eastern Milk Snake
- ☐ Eastern Tiger Salamander
- ☐ Five-lined Skink
- ☐ Northern Leopard Frog
- ☐ Northern Map Turtle
- ☐ Plains Spadefoot Toad
- ☐ Spiny Softshell Turtle
- ☐ Spring Peeper
- ☐ Timber Rattlesnake
- ☐ Western Slender Glass Lizard

The Art of Conservation®

Featuring two signature programs, The Songbird Art Contest™ and The Fish Art Contest®, the Art of Conservation programs celebrate the arts as a cornerstone to conservation. To enter, youth artists create an original hand-drawn illustration and written essay, story, or poem synthesizing what they have learned. The contests are FREE and open to students in K-12. For program updates, rules, guidelines, and entry forms, visit: www.TheArtofConservation.org.

The Fish Art Contest® introduces youth to the wonders of fish, the joy of fishing, and the importance of aquatic conservation. The Fish Art Contest uses art, science, and creative writing to foster connections to the outdoors and inspire the next generation of stewards. Participants are encouraged to use the Fish On! lesson plan, then submit an original, handmade piece of artwork to compete for prizes and international recognition.

The Songbird Art Contest® explores the wonders and species diversity of North American songbirds. Raising awareness and educating the public on bird conservation, the Songbird program builds stewardship, encourages outdoors participation, and promotes the discovery of nature as close as anyone's backyard.

Photo Credits

About the Author

Alex Troutman is a wildlife biologist, birder, nature enthusiast, and science communicator from Austell, Georgia. He has a passion for sharing the wonders of nature and introducing the younger generation to the outdoors. He holds both a bachelor's degree and a master's degree in biology from Georgia Southern University (the Real GSU), with a focus in conservation. Because he knows what it feels like to not see individuals who look like you (or come from a similar background) doing the things you enjoy or working in the career that you aspire to be in, Alex makes a point not only to be that representation for the younger generation, but also to make sure that kids have exposure to the careers they are interested in and the diverse scientists working in those careers.

Alex is the co-organizer of several Black in X weeks, including Black Birders Week, Black Mammologists Week, and Black in Marine Science Week. This movement encourages diversity in nature, the celebration of Black individual scientists, awareness of Black nature enthusiasts, and diversity in STEAM fields.

ABOUT ADVENTUREKEEN

We are an independent nature and outdoor activity publisher. Our founding dates back more than 40 years, guided then and now by our love of being in the woods and on the water, by our passion for reading and books, and by the sense of wonder and discovery made possible by spending time recreating outdoors in beautiful places. It is our mission to share that wonder and fun with our readers, especially with those who haven't yet experienced all the physical and mental health benefits that nature and outdoor activity can bring. #bewellbeoutdoors